avp   op 6⁰⁰

D1443532

Critique of Stammler

Max Weber

Translated, with an introductory essay, by Guy Oakes

THE FREE PRESS
A Division of Macmillan, Inc.
NEW YORK

Maxwell Macmillan Canada
TORONTO

Maxwell Macmillan International
NEW YORK   OXFORD   SINGAPORE   SYDNEY

The Free Press
A Division of Macmillan, Inc.
866 Third Avenue, New York, N.Y. 10022

Maxwell Macmillan Canada, Inc.
1200 Eglinton Avenue East
Suite 200
Don Mills, Ontario M3C 3N1

Macmillan, Inc. is part of the Maxwell Communication Group of Companies.

Printed in the United States of America

printing number

2 3 4 5 6 7 8 9 10

Library of Congress Cataloging in Publication Data

Weber, Max, 1864–1920.
    Critique of Stammler.

    Translation of R. Stammler's 'Überwindung' der materialistischen Geschichtsauffassung.
    Extended critical review of the 2d ed. of Rudolf Stammler's Wirtschaft und Recht nach der materialistischen Geschichtsauffassung.
    Bibliography: p.
    Includes index.
    1. Stammler, Rudolf, 1856–1938.   Wirtschaft und Recht nach der materialistischen Geschichtsauffassung.
2. Sociology. 3. Economics. 4. Historical materialism. 5. Law—Philosophy. I. Title.
HM24.W4213   1977   300'.1   77-72682
ISBN 0-02-934100-0

Contents

Preface

Max Weber's colleagues and friends included men as idiosyncratically different—and arrogant—as Ernst Troeltsch, Heinrich Rickert, and Georg Simmel. Troeltsch was a Heidelberg historian and theologian who shared Weber's interests in the history and sociology of religion. For a number of years, he also shared Weber's house on the Ziegelhäuser Landstrasse overlooking the Neckar. Rickert was a neo-Kantian academic philosopher who had known Weber since they were both children in Berlin. They became colleagues at Freiburg, where Rickert was a *Dozent* in philosophy and Weber held his first professorship. Later Rickert followed Weber to Heidelberg, where he studied the development of Weber's methodological work carefully. Simmel was the great virtuoso of the sociocultural sciences. Sociologist, epistemologist, aesthetician, and intellectual historian, for most of his career he remained an untenured lecturer at Berlin. Simmel was a regular visitor at Weber's home in Heidelberg, and he and Weber corresponded frequently. Weber lobbied, unsuccessfully, to secure a professorship for Simmel at Heidelberg. Weber's three friends were not given to false modesty, misplaced humility, or a lavish generosity in the estimation of the abilities of their contemporary colleagues, virtues which apparently were neither encouraged nor rewarded in the intellectual culture of Wilhelminian Germany. Yet all three recognized Weber as a genius.

Rickert and Karl Jaspers, who did not seem to agree on any other issue—including the question of whether Jaspers should be appointed to a chair in philosophy at Heidelberg—both described Weber as the greatest German thinker of their era. From the perspective of its clarity, originality, and historical importance, Jaspers suggests, Weber's methodology is comparable to Galileo's work on the foundations of the natural sciences. Rickert also introduces a comparison between Weber's methodological writings and the works on the philosophy of science produced by the natural philosophers of the Renaissance. Bacon, Galileo, and Descartes worked in the philosophy of science in order to clarify new methods for investigating natural phenomena. Their writings acquired a fundamental importance for later generations of natural scientists and achieved a classical status. According to Rickert, the intention behind Weber's methodological work was also to develop a "new organon," a new logic of sociocultural research, a new paradigm or problematic which would define the subject matter, problems, methods, and theoretical aims of the sociocultural sciences.

Max Weber published his first methodological essay seventy four years ago. All of Weber's methodological writings were collected and published fifty five years ago. Where do we stand in relation to Max Weber's methodology? According to Weber himself, it is the fate of any piece of scientific research or scholarship to become antiquated within fifty years. This is a consequence of the immanent dialectic of scientific progress and the increasing sophistication of the division of scientific labor. Have the consequences of Max Weber's methodology been understood and fully exploited? Have its limits and defects been exposed and analyzed? Have the sociocultural sciences comprehended, tested, criticized, exhausted, and transcended the possibilities of Weber's methodology? Do we see further than Max Weber because we are standing on the shoulders of a giant? Or—to employ the version of this metaphor used by Bernard of Chartres in his description of the relationship between the scholars of the twelfth century and the philosophers of antiquity—are we at least dwarfs sitting on the shoulders of a giant? Advanced work on the history of the sociocultural sciences is not required to appreciate the rhetorical character of these questions. Our position in relation to the methodological work of Max Weber is much more modest. We have the perspective of dwarfs gazing into the inscrutable visage of a distant and towering colossus. Bernard knew that the works of his contemporaries could not be compared to the achievements of the ancients. But he also knew that he had studied their writings carefully and critically. However large and important portions of Weber's methodology and the works of others who influenced him—in particular, the writings of Dilthey, Simmel, and Rickert—have remained inaccessible to Anglo-American students of the sociocultural sciences because they have remained untranslated.

As a result of the enterprise of The Free Press and its editor-in-chief, Charles E. Smith, a more complete exposition of the methodology on which "interpretive" social science rests is now available. In 1975, The Free Press published Weber's first and most ambitious methodological work: *Roscher and Knies: The Logical Problems of Historical Economics.* This was followed by a translation of Simmel's most comprehensive work in the philosophy of the sociocultural sciences, *The Problems of the Philosophy of History,* a book Weber often cites as an important source of his own views. The present translation of Weber's critique of Stammler reveals a number of crucial links. It exposes the connections between the Roscher–Knies monograph and the problematic of *Economy and Society,* and it also reveals the intimate relationship between Weber's methodology and a number of contemporary methodologies: the overlapping theories of ethnomethodology, phenomenological sociology, hermeneutical sociology, and the sociology of everyday life. Each of these translations was improved by intelligent and literate revisions introduced by Eileen Fitzgerald DeWald, midwife of these manuscripts at The Free Press. The research on which the translations are based was supported by three grants from Monmouth College.

Introductory Essay

Guy Oakes

Weber's text

The text translated below is Max Weber's extended critical review of the second edition of Rudolf Stammler's book *The Historical Materialist Conception of Economy and Law: A Sociophilosophical Investigation* (1906). At the time Weber wrote his critique, Stammler (1856-1938) was a professor at Halle. Later he was called to Berlin, the premier university of the Wilhelminian Reich. Here he held one of the most prestigious chairs in the German university system and became one of the most influential legal scholars of his time. Stammler's academic reputation was based on several works in jurisprudence (Stammler, 1902, 1911, 1922). The first edition of *Economy and Law* appeared in 1896. Stammler conceived it as an epistemological inquiry into the foundations of social science. The social sciences, Stammler tells us, are in a state of vacillation and confusion. The uncertain

1

status of social science, Stammler thinks, poses the following questions. Can lawlike regularities within social life be established, regularities that are comparable to the laws of nature that constitute the foundations of the natural sciences? Or are there fundamental differences between social life and nature? And if essential differences between nature and social life can be identified, to what extent is it justifiable to apply the methods and the conceptual apparatus of the natural sciences to the problems of the social sciences? In order to resolve these questions, Stammler claims, a philosophical investigation is necessary, an investigation which would resolve the following problem. "What are the basic and formal nomological conditions on which *human* social life rests" (Stammler, 1921, pp. 6-7)? The solution to this problem will identify the concepts and the principles that constitute the logical conditions for the possibility of social science. This philosophical inquiry, according to Stammler, requires an analysis of the concept of social life. This is the "constitutive concept"—the *"Grundbegriff"*—of the social sciences (Stammler, 1921, p. 10). Therefore any attempt to establish the epistemological foundations of the social sciences must begin with the analysis of this concept. What is social life? What are its constitutive properties? Under what conditions can a given item be conceived as a social phenomenon?

Stammler poses these questions in the "Introduction" to his book, which is entitled *"Sozialphilosophie."* This might be translated as "philosophy of social science." We find his answers in Book Two of the treatise, called "The Object of Social Science." In chapter one ("Human Social Life"), section 16 ("The Concept of Society") of Book Two, Stammler instructs the reader as follows. First, it is obvious that the concept of the social coexistence of men is both "different" from and "more inclusive" than the concept of the given, empirical, spatio-temporal existence of men. The concept of social life refers to a certain mode of coexistence that can be distinguished from the mere fact that individual human beings, conceived as objects in the natural world, coexist in the same spatio-temporal frame. What is the "conceptual" difference between this latter sort of existence—"a purely physical coexistence"—and "collective societal life"?

"At this point, the decisive factor that we are searching for appears, the criterion that defines *social life as a special object of knowledge*" (Stammler, 1921, p. 81). What is this criterion? What is the definitive property of social life? "This criterion is the regulation of human intercourse and collective life on the basis of rules which men themselves have instituted" (Stammler, 1921, p. 81).

The *external* or *observable regulation* of human conduct is a necessary condition for the possibility of *the concept* of social life as a distinctive object. It is the ultimate criterion on which any conception of the *social* as such formally rests. Consider the *definitive* conceptual *synthesis* which constitutes social science as a distinctive and objective form of knowledge. The external regulation of human collective life is a necessary condition for the possibility of this synthesis (Stammler, 1921, p. 81).

In other words, as Stammler summarizes this discussion, "*social* life is the *externally regulated* collective life of human beings" (Stammler, 1921, p. 82). Put another way, rules are the constitutive phenomena of the social sciences. The fact that it is rule-governed is the property of a phenomenon which defines it as an object of social science.[1]

The essential facts concerning the publication of Weber's critique of Stammler are the following. Weber published the first four parts in the *Archiv für Sozialwissenschaft und Sozialpolitik,* volume 24, 1907, under the title "R. Stammler's 'Refutation' of the Materialist Conception of History."[2] This essay concludes with a footnote: "Another article will follow." This is a familiar note to students of Max Weber's metatheoretical work. The three-part monograph on Roscher and Knies and the Historical School of economics ends with the same line. But the concluding essay never appeared. The monograph remains—as Weber himself describes it in his preface—a "fragment." The same holds for the monograph on Eduard Meyer. "A further article will follow," Weber promised. But the work was never completed.[3] However a conclusion, or at least a sequel, to the 1907 essay was written. Johannes Winckelmann, Marianne Weber's successor as the German editor of Weber's works, describes it as a "draft" and an "incomplete sequel" (Weber, 1968, p. 359n. 1). After Weber's death, Marianne found it among his unpublished papers. In 1921, the year after Weber's death, Stammler published a fourth edition of *Economy and Law*. In a long note, he responds to some of Weber's criticisms (Stammler, 1921, pp. 670-673). He begins with an allusion to the fragmentary character of Weber's essay: "It is certainly not the model of a clear refutation" (Stammler, 1921, p. 670). He intimates that it is not easy to discover exactly what critical points Weber wants to make and concludes with a reference to the inconclusiveness of Weber's paper. "The critique was broken off after the first article. It was not completed" (Stammler, 1921, p. 673). In 1922, Marianne published a collection of Weber's metatheoretical works under the title *Gesammelte Aufsätze zur Wissenschaftslehre*.[4] Among them was a reprint of the 1907 article. The sequel was published here for the first time as "Nachtrag zu dem Aufsatz über R. Stammler's 'Überwindung' der materialistischen Geschichtsauffassung" (Postscript to the Essay on R. Stammler's "Refutation" of the Materialist Conception of History). This comprises the last two sections of the monograph. Three subsequent editions of the *Wissenschaftslehre*, each including a reprint of the monograph, were published in 1950, 1968, and 1974, under the editorship of Johannes Winckelmann. These four editions of the monograph are substantively indistinguishable. The editions of 1922 and 1968 were used for this translation.

Weber divided the monograph into sections and subsections. The divisions he employed and the titles he gave them are reproduced in the Contents. All emphases are Weber's. He regularly employs a variety of techniques of emphasis for rhetorical purposes. When Weber wants to stress the importance of an expression, he places it in italics. In his "Preliminary Remarks," for example, Weber stresses the words "second edition." This is because he wants the reader to note the following point. Weber's criticisms of Stammler are severe and unqualified. But they should be. He is not criticizing an experimental, programmatic draft but, rather, a text which the author had ample opportunity to correct and revise. When Weber wants to question the import of an expression, he places it within quotation marks. In the title of the 1907 essay, for example, the word "refutation" is placed in quotation marks because Weber does not believe that Stammler's book qualifies as a refutation of historical materialism. When Weber thinks that Stammler is making a suspicious, unwarranted, surreptitious, or false move—and this is often what Weber thinks—he draws the reader's attention to this move by the use of the device "(note!)." When Weber thinks that Stammler is making a move that is inexplicable, advocating a thesis that is incomprehensible, or employing a concept that is unintelligible, he uses the device "(?)." When Weber thinks that Stammler has made a claim that is obviously false, self-contradictory, self-defeating, or inconsistent with some other claim that Stammler has made, he uses the device "(!)." Weber sometimes uses these devices within quoted material. In other words, he breaks up quotations from Stammler's text with these techniques of emphasis and parenthetical remarks of his own. If Weber's intentions are understood, it is easy enough to follow his use of these devices. Their purpose is not to confuse or bewilder the reader. On the contrary, Weber wants to help the reader understand Stammler's views, views that he regards as ambiguous, confused, and obscure. His strategy, therefore, is to guide the reader, to focus his attention, and to encourage him to doubt. Weber, Pirandello-like, sometimes interposes himself between his text and his reader. In these contexts, his aim is to serve as a midwife of interpretation.

In the German editions of the monograph, Weber's notes are placed at the foot of the page. The notes here have been numbered serially and placed at the end of the text. The bibliographical standards of Weber and his contemporaries were more informal than our own. Date and place of publication are often omitted in Weber's citations. The present translation provides more complete bibliographical information concerning the principal works Weber cites.

Weber's metatheoretical work easily lends itself to exegetical thought, the form assumed by most of the secondary literature on his methodology. The problematical features of Weber's scholarly prose are at least partially responsible for this, features that have been stressed repeatedly by commentators, translators, and critics. These difficulties were also noticed by Weber's contemporaries, even by those closest to him. Marianne suggests that the style of Weber's methodological work created the impression that he willfully neglected his scholarly prose. She also reports that Rickert, upon reading the 1907 essay, complained about its stylistic difficulties and the demands it places upon the reader. Rickert was a professional academic philosopher. In addition, he and Weber understood the same language. This included not only the academic German of the philosophical faculties, but also the vocabulary of the *Methodenstreiten*, the technical language of the various controversies that developed in the German sociocultural sciences during the three decades before World War I. This language is no longer fully intelligible. It can be retrieved, within modest limits, by the specialized scholar of late nineteenth century German intellectual life. Finally, Rickert had known Weber well since the early 1890s, and he was thoroughly familiar with Weber's work. Indeed, he regarded Weber's metatheoretical studies as an extension of his own ideas. If Rickert found the task of reading the critique of Stammler unreasonably difficult, where does that leave *us*?

As a matter of fact, Weber's metatheoretical works would impose extraordinary demands upon the reader even if they did not employ a complex, eclectic, and archaic conceptual apparatus. Weber has a notorious tendency to cast his arguments within long, tortuous, and convoluted sentences. One dependent clause is encased within another. The sentence may be broken up by parenthetical remarks, ironical asides, reservations, questions, and instructions to the reader. And it may be followed by a reference to a note of several hundred words which reproduces all the difficulties of the sentence itself. Although some of Weber's arguments are fatiguingly long, others are quite brief, merely sketches of arguments. The reader is obliged to fill in premises that Weber has only implied or suggested. Finally, there are passages in which Weber moves rapidly and surprisingly from one collection of problems to another, supplying only a perfunctory explanatory transition, or no transition at all. Yet there is manifest evidence that Weber was a gifted polemicist and a superb lecturer.[5] Further, writings like *The Protestant Ethic and the Spirit of Capitalism* and the two Munich lectures on science and politics show that Weber was the master of a remarkably idiosyncratic prose in which acute analytical penetration and an encyclopedic breadth of knowledge do not exclude irony, pathos, and brilliant exercises in metaphor. Can the Max Weber who wrote the serpentine essays on Knies be the same Max Weber who wrote the concluding chapter of *The Protestant Ethic*?

How can this discrepancy be explained? Marianne's account runs as follows. Commenting on the composition of the Roscher-Knies monograph—Weber called the Roscher essay the "*Seufzeraufsatz*," a "work of sheer torture"—she says:

> Like several other methodological treatises, he simply did not complete it. New tasks pressed themselves upon him, and a convalescent like Weber, who recovered only very slowly and whose capacity for work continued to waver for years, required, in his own opinion, increasingly novel motivations to overcome the impediments of his illness. What he did and the manner in which he presented it were all the same to him, if he was simply able to work (Marianne Weber, 1926, p. 319).

In addition, Weber wanted to make these works as brief as possible, and he wanted to complete them as quickly as possible. For he "was repeatedly compelled to take up new substantive problems" (Marianne Weber, p. 319). Finally: "Weber gave no attention to the systematic presentation of the results of his thought. He had no desire to be an academic logician. The form in which the wealth of his ideas appeared was quite without importance to him" (Marianne Weber, 1926, p. 322). Weber's unpolished methodological style, therefore, is a consequence of his prolonged illness, his inability to concentrate on conceptual problems for extended periods of time, his impatience to return to the investigation of substantive problems, and his indifference to questions of literary form. The problem, however, is more complicated than this explanation suggests. Weber was committed to a theory of rhetoric which led him to make rigorous distinctions between different kinds of discourse. He often calls the principle of this theory of rhetoric "*Sachlichkeit*." *Sachlichkeit* is a certain kind of objectivity. But it should not be confused with detachment, impartiality, or dispassionate indifference. The scholar who has *Sachlichkeit* is committed, but he is not committed to his personality, his career, or his style. He is committed to his *Sache*: the object of his interest, the matter at issue, the requirements of his discipline—what Weber sometimes calls "the demands of the day." The thinker who is *sachlich* is objective in the following sense: he is detached from himself and all other considerations that do not bear upon his *Sache*, the interest to which he is committed. The place for the perfection of a literary technique is the literary work itself. The place for autobiographical confessions is the confessional—it is not difficult to imagine Weber's response to the contemporary fashion in the sociocultural sciences which allows or even encourages the intrusion of the personality of the social scientist into the work of analysis and argument. The place for sermonizing is the pulpit. The place for the declaration and defense of values is the orator's platform. The place for a facile style and literary polemics is the popular journal. But what does the interest of methodological work require? Above all, intellectual honesty and careful, perspicuous analysis. If, for example, the various distinctions between the natural and the sociocultural sciences are unclear, incomplete, and fundamentally confused, then it is the obligation of the methodologist to analyze and clarify this state of affairs. If the fundamental concepts of the sociocultural sciences are ambiguous, then the task of the methodologist is to trace these ambiguities. If the extratheoretical interests of the sociocultural sciences form a battleground on which the various gods, demons, or axiological commitments of our culture struggle for ascendancy, then the problem of the methodologist is to provide an accurate conceptual map of this terrain which does not conceal or oversimplify the sources of its complexity. In Weber's view, the conditions for the adequacy of such a methodology may exclude a facile prose, make ease of comprehension impossible, and rule out ideally rigorous standards of precision, clear and distinct ideas, exhaustive distinctions, and complete solutions.

This is not to suggest that Weber's metatheoretical work satisfies these conditions. In the critique of Stammler, the distinction between a discourse which employs polemics and invective and a discourse which excludes these rhetorical techniques in the interest of perspicuous logic threatens to break down. However, the foregoing considerations are sufficient to explain the discrepancies between the various styles of discourse which Weber employs without recourse to the following extravagant hypothesis: the awkward and unpolished style of much of Weber's metatheoretical writing is evidence of his relative indifference to methodological issues (see Tenbruck, 1959, p. 583).

Weber's Methodological Problematic

Between 1903 and 1918, Weber published eight major essays on the methodology of the sociocultural sciences. Six of these essays appeared during an interval of five years. In 1903, Weber published a paper entitled "Roscher's 'Historical Method'" (Weber, 1903). This was his first purely methodological essay, a critique of the metatheoretical—and, especially metaphysical—assumptions of the German Historical School of economics. The famous programmatic essay on the "objectivity" of social science followed in 1904 (Weber, 1904). In 1905, the first essay on Knies appeared (Weber, 1905). This forms the second part of the Roscher-Knies monograph. In the two Knies essays, the arguments of the Roscher paper are expanded to include a critique of intuitionist theories of sociocultural knowledge, a critique of various ontological distinctions between the natural and the sociocultural sciences, and a general sketch of the definitive logical properties of the sociocultural sciences. In 1906, Weber published two major methodological writings: the second essay on Knies and the monograph on Eduard Meyer (Weber, 1906a, 1906b). The essay on Stammler followed in 1907. Weber also wrote shorter review articles that focused on metatheoretical problems, and he was constantly embroiled in methodological disputes. Yet he remained quite skeptical about the value of methodological work. Why?[6]

First, an emphasis on methodological issues invites "dilettantism," one of Weber's favorite words for the expression of contempt. The social scientist is not well schooled in the use of the technical concepts employed by logicians and methodologists of science. In Weber's view, this is an inevitable consequence of the intensive specialization required by the increasingly sophisticated division of scientific labor. Suppose that a social scientist attempts to analyze some metatheoretical problem posed by his discipline. In employing the conceptual apparatus of the professional methodologist, he is apt to commit ludicrous and sophomoric errors, mistakes that are a result of his ineptitude in the use of these concepts. There is a clear statement of this view at the beginning of the critique of Stammler. Weber describes Stammler as a professional jurist and philosophical dilettante who had the bad judgment to dabble in epistemology. A second reason for Weber's skepticism about the value of methodological work: "Something like a methodological pestilence," Weber claims, "prevails within our discipline" (Weber, 1964, p. 139). One methodological work begets not only another, but an entire generation of methodological works: commentaries, expositions, critiques, and refutations. They, in turn, produce a new and even larger generation of methodological writings. The result is a methodological pestilence. But what is the justification for representing a voluminous methodological literature as a plague? The answer to this question identifies Weber's third reason for skepticism about the value of methodological work. The definitive problems of the sociocultural sciences are empirical. They can be resolved only within the domain of substantive sociocultural theory.

> Sciences are founded and their methods are progressively developed only when *substantive* problems are discovered and solved. Purely epistemological or methodological reflections have never yet made a decisive contribution to this project (Weber, 1968, p. 217).

The claim that methodological work is a necessary condition for fruitful scientific research is false. This is the anti-Cartesian turn in Weber's methodological thought. In his view, an inquiry into the foundations of knowledge is not, in general, essential to successful scientific research. According to Weber, methodology will prove to be valuable only when something has gone wrong in the pursuit of research. Weber compares the social scientist who has methodological problems with a patient who is sick or diseased. Suppose that there is some sense in which the sociocultural sciences are sick or diseased. Under these conditions, the social scientist will apply his knowledge of methodology to produce a cure. Or he will prepare a description of the symptoms of his disease and consult a methodological specialist who can be expected to recommend the proper therapy. Weber uses this analogy at the beginning of the monograph on Eduard Meyer. He describes Meyer's epistemological reflections as a "description of an illness" or a "diagnostic report." It is not the doctor's description, but rather the report of the patient himself. The patient does not prescribe a cure. The medical specialist is responsible for that. Eduard Meyer, in describing the "diseased" state of the sociocultural sciences, does not recommend a therapy. He only provides an account of what has gone wrong. Who prescribes the cure for the disease of Eduard Meyer and his contemporaries? The methodologist.[7]

Between 1903 and 1907, Weber was intensively engaged in two kinds of methodological work. Both can be described in the language of his analogy. He attempted to diagnose the "disease" of the sociocultural sciences: the *Methodenstreit*, the methodological controversy which in his generation had reached the proportions of a crisis. And he attempted to prescribe a cure by showing how the constitutive issues of the *Methodenstreit* could be resolved. It follows that Weber must have thought that the sociocultural sciences were, in some sense, sick or diseased. What had gone wrong?

Weber never attempts to answer this question in a systematic fashion. However, his various responses to it, scattered throughout his essays, are very close in both substance and language. The methods of the sociocultural sciences, their conceptual constructs, and the criteria for the validity of these constructs are in a state of "constant flux." They are the subject of "embittered controversy" (Weber, 1968, pp. 147-148). Weber conceives the sociocultural disciplines as an arena in which a "struggle over methods, 'basic concepts' and presuppositions" is waged. The result is a "perpetual flux of 'problematics' and a constant redefinition of 'concepts' " (Weber, 1968, pp. 160-161). Consider the "normal" state of specialized research in the sociocultural sciences. The scholar—perhaps unwittingly—employs a specific problematic, a certain set of presuppositions, or, to employ the term which has been in vogue for several years, a paradigm. This problematic constitutes an unquestioned, although not unquestionable, set of assumptions. These assumptions supply answers to the following questions. How is the subject matter of the sociocultural sciences to be identified? What constitutes a sociocultural problem? How should a sociocultural investigation proceed? What qualifies as a solution to a sociocultural problem? From the standpoint of such a problematic, the solution to specific substantive problems is "an end in itself." The scholar does not see himself as obliged to question the ultimate value of the results he establishes and the discoveries he makes. He may not even be aware of the fact that his own work is grounded or "anchored" in certain unquestioned ideas of value (Weber, 1968, p. 214). However, this Baconian utopia of scientific research is fragile. No problematic is unquestionable. "Eventually the light will fade. The significance of those problematics which were unreflectively employed becomes dubious. We lose our way in the twilight. The light which illuminates the great cultural problems shifts. When this happens, the sciences also prepare to alter their status and change their conceptual apparatus" (Weber, 1968, p. 214). Conceptual schemes in the sociocultural sciences have their moments of youth, maturity, and decline, their periods of dawn, day, and dusk. The social scientist who has lost his way in the twilight—the scholar who no longer has confidence in his own conceptual apparatus— can no longer treat the solution to specific substantive problems as intrinsically valuable. On the contrary, he has become skeptical about the value or point of his own research. Because of his skepticism, he is compelled "to look down from the pinnacle of thought into the flux of events" (Weber, 1968, p. 214). Put less dramatically, he is obliged to question the value of his own problematic.[8]

Suppose that these conditions are satisfied. In other words:

> Suppose that radical shifts in the points of view which constitute any item as an object of investigation have taken place. Suppose that, as a result of these shifts, the idea arises that the new "points of view" also require a revision of the logic of scientific research that has hitherto prevailed within the discipline. And suppose that the result of all of this is uncertainty about the "essential purpose" of one's own scientific work. It is incontestable that the historical disciplines now find themselves in this predicament (Weber, 1968, p. 218).

Under these conditions, it is necessary for the social scientist to become a methodologist. In Weber's view, this is the preeminent value of methodology in the sociocultural sciences: its purpose is to resolve crises generated by the conflicts of conceptual schemes.[9] If methodology is successful in a period of crisis and skepticism, it will resolve the confusion of the scholar who is lost, uncertain about the "essential purpose" of his work, and suspended between the "twilight" of one conceptual scheme and the "dawn" of another. Under these circumstances—conditions of crisis that Weber regards as extraordinary—methodological work seems to be essential to the progress of sociocultural research.

Weber, therefore, writing in the decade before World War I, sees the sociocultural sciences as a battleground where conflicting conceptual schemes struggle for domination. This conflict, in his view, is an aspect of the polytheism of values that is characteristic of modernity: the implacable struggle between the various "gods" or "demons" of modern culture. The result is a protracted crisis in sociocultural research. How did Weber reach this conclusion? In his view, what was responsible for the contemporary predicament of the sociocultural sciences? What radical shifts had occurred in the conceptual frameworks within which the social world is constituted as an object of scientific investigation? Why did the logic of sociocultural research require revision? Why was skepticism about the definitive aims of sociocultural science so prevalent? Why had the social scientist lost his way in the twilight? In other words, what generated this crisis? This is a way of posing the problem: What were the definitive issues of the *Methodenstreit* as Weber saw them? In view of Weber's encyclopedic education, a full answer to this question would require an extensive analysis of the development of the sociocultural sciences in Germany during the nineteenth century. Such an analysis is not available at this point.[10] The following brief remarks on the logic of the *Methodenstreit* represent only an attempt to sketch the problematic within which Weber's methodology developed. This problematic may be identified as a certain set of metatheoretical issues which, in Weber's view, constituted or defined the *Methodenstreit*. The critique of Stammler focuses upon one of these issues. Taken as a whole, Weber's methodological work can be conceived as an attempt to resolve each of these issues and thereby to terminate the *Methodenstreit*.

From the standpoint of Weber's methodological work, the following issues may be identified as the definitive problems of the *Methodenstreit*. (1) The controversy over the constitutive properties of sociocultural phenomena: What is a sociocultural fact? What are the criteria for the identification of these facts? What are the distinguishing features of the subject matter of the sociocultural sciences? What conditions must any item satisfy in order to qualify as a sociocultural phenomenon? (2) The controversy over the domain of sociocultural problems: Within the sociocultural sciences, what constitutes a problem? How are the problems of these sciences to be defined? What are their distinguishing features? (3) The controversy over the theoretical purpose or "interest" (Weber's word) of the sociocultural sciences: What is a solution to a sociocultural problem? What conditions should such a solution satisfy? Another way of posing this question: What criteria must any account satisfy in order to qualify as a successful sociocultural theory? (4) The controversy over method: Is there a definitive set of "rules of sociological method"? What is the logic of sociocultural research? According to what principles should a sociocultural investigation proceed?

A convenient beginning point for a discussion of the *Methodenstreit* and an excellent illustration of its logic—the circumstances under which these four constitutive issues arose and the consequences of their problematical status—is the dispute between Carl Menger and Gustav Schmoller. In this debate, Weber claims, "the temperature of the methodological controversy in economics reached its highest point" (Weber, 1975, p. 94). In 1883, Menger, a professor at Vienna, published his *Investigations concerning the Method of the Social Sciences with special Reference to Economics*. As Menger describes it, his book is concerned with the "nature" of economics: its domain, the logical status of its propositions, and the purposes of its investigations (Menger, 1883, p. x). The principal argument of the book is an extended polemic against the German Historical School of economics. Menger begins with a few reflections on the purposes and limits of methodology in the sociocultural sciences (Menger, 1883, pp. x-xii). In both substance and language, these observations are very close to Weber's remarks on the same subject, close enough to support the inference that Weber adopted Menger's position on the uses of methodology as his own. Menger claims that he does not want to exaggerate the importance of methodology for empirical research. There is, he says, an "immeasurable distance" between the results of methodology and the actual established structure of an empirical science. The most significant scientific discoveries have been made by scientists who had no interest in methodological problems. And the greatest methodologists have often proven to be extremely unproductive in the area of empirical research. Sciences have frequently been founded or transformed by a form of empirical research that was not grounded on any sophisticated methodology. But purely methodological work has never created or revolutionized any science. If we examine the main problems of any science, therefore, we shall see that methodology plays only a very modest role in their solution. According to Menger, there is only one circumstance in which methodology acquires a preeminent status. Suppose that the scientists who work within a given discipline have lost the proper perception of the real purposes of research, purposes that are determined by the nature of the subject matter of that particular science. Suppose that the "subsidiary" or "secondary" problems of this science acquire an exaggerated significance. Perhaps they are even conceived of as the definitive problems of the discipline. Suppose that false methodological doctrines advocated by powerful academic interests acquire a predominant influence. In other words, suppose that the progress of a science is impeded by the force of false but fundamental methodological doctrines. Under these conditions, methodological work is essential to scientific progress. Therefore the practicing scientist, who would otherwise prefer to spend his time investigating the real substantive problems of his discipline, is obliged to enter the methodological controversy. As a matter of fact, Menger claims, this is the predicament of the social sciences—and especially economics—in Germany. German social science, he says, is in a state of "demoralization" or "decadence"—in his characterizations of the influence of the Historical School, Menger favors the language of demoralization, corruption, and decay. Under these circumstances, what conclusions should the social scientist draw? "At this point, false methodological doctrines constitute an obstacle to the progress of our science. Therefore methodological work is now of principal importance" (Menger, 1883, p. xix). Methodology will retain this preeminent status until these pernicious methodological doctrines are refuted. This project of refutation, Menger claims, requires an analysis of the definitive methods and theoretical interests of the social sciences.

The Historical School, according to Menger, misconceives the subject matter of economics as history. It misrepresents the problems of economic theory as historical problems. From the standpoint of the Historical School, research in economics is historical research. An economic inquiry and an historical inquiry have the same logic and the same purpose. According to Menger, the Historical School is mistaken. Economics is not an historical discipline. The discipline of history does not exhaust the problems of the social sciences in general. In relation to theoretical social science, history is only an "auxiliary discipline," a "Hilfswissenschaft" (Menger, 1883, p. 18). Theoretical social science and historical research are independent enterprises. They have logically distinguishable objects of investigation and different problems, methods, and purposes. Menger defends a conception of economic theory that has two purposes. One of its aims is to discover "real types"—"the basic forms of empirical phenomena"—and "empirical laws" (Menger, 1883, p. 36). This is the sort of theorizing that Menger calls "realistic-empirical." The purpose of this sort of theory is to discover the strict and universal laws according to which empirical phenomena function. Menger admits that "phenomena in their full empirical reality" may not actually conform to these laws. In other words, it may not be possible to deduce these laws from any set of observation statements, no matter how complete they may be. However, these "exact laws" explain the relationships which obtain in empirical reality (Menger, 1883, p. 43).

Menger's exact laws of economics are comparable to the laws of motion in classical mechanics. The laws of motion cannot be deduced from any set of observation statements concerning the mass, position, and velocity of a body. However, the experimentally established values of these variables can be explained by reference to the laws of motion. In Menger's view, therefore, the subject matter of economics is constituted by transhistorical or ahistorically defined "types" or "forms" of economic phenomena. The definitive problems of economics are comparable to the problems of mechanics: How can the properties of these complex phenomena be explained by reference to abstract and exact laws which reduce these phenomena to their simplest elements? The methods and theoretical purposes of the social sciences, therefore, are essentially the same as the methods and purposes of mechanics.

Menger did not have to wait long for an early and major review of his book. In 1883, Gustav Schmoller reviewed it in *Jahrbuch für Gesetzgebung, Verwaltung und Volkswirtschaft—Schmoller's Jahrbuch,* at the time the major academic journal for sociocultural science in Germany. Schmoller, a Berlin historian and economist, was the editor of the journal, a leader of the Historical School, and one of the most powerful *Kathedersozialisten*—the "academic socialists" or "socialists of the lectern." His review remains a curiosity in the history of the professional literature of social science. The first volume of Wilhelm Dilthey's ambitious attempt to provide a Kantian critique of historical reason also appeared in 1883: *Introduction to the Sociocultural Sciences.* In one article of twenty pages, Schmoller attempted to review both of these books—each a complex, original, and extremely demanding work. Dilthey receives ten pages of superficial commentary and wishes of good luck on his project. "However in the case of Menger," Schmoller explains, "I cannot avoid polemics altogether. This is because his attacks in part concern me personally" (Schmoller, 1883, p. 239). Schmoller defends the problematic of the Historical School. "In the future, economics will enjoy a new epoch, but only by employing the entire corpus of historical-descriptive and statistical material that is being gathered now. This new epoch will not be a result of further redistillation of the abstract theorems of the old dogmatics, propositions which have already been distilled hundreds of times" (Schmoller, 1883, p. 242). The "old dogmatics" refers to the economic theories of Adam Smith, David Ricardo, and their German followers, a problematic often identified in the Historical School by the use of the epithet "Manchestertum" or "Manchesterism." This is a pejorative term that was intended to suggest a utilitarian ethics, a laissez-faire politics, and a positivist methodology; in other words, a problematic that the Historical School found objectionable on ethical, political, and methodological grounds. Menger's exact laws are dismissed as "illusory phantoms" and "vain imaginings" (Schmoller, 1883, p. 244), "abstract, nebulous images that have absolutely no real status" (Schmoller, 1883, p. 247). Menger himself is described as a logician and a clever dialectician who lacks the "universal philosophical and historical education" that his project requires (Schmoller, 1883, p. 251). He is dismissed as "an epigone who has been schooled exclusively in Mill's logic of the natural sciences and the archaic, abstract dogmatics of classical economics" (Schmoller, 1883, p. 251). In Schmoller's view, therefore, the subject matter of economics is constituted by historically defined economic phenomena. The definitive problems of economics are historical problems: the collection and confirmation of historical facts. The purpose and method of economics are essentially the same as the purpose and method of history: the "reproduction" of economic or historical reality by means of increasingly exact and exhaustive historical descriptions (Schmoller, 1883, p. 242).[11]

The interest in the dispute between Menger and Schmoller does not lie in the value of their solutions to the problems debated, solutions which are very inadequately set forth. The vagueness of their principal theses and the extremely modest level of conceptual precision which the debate attains confused their contemporaries and successors. Menger and Schmoller contributed to the *Methodenstreit* by increasing the number of controverted issues. Exactly what did Menger mean? Did Schmoller really understand him? Was Schmoller's review accurate, justified, mistaken, irrelevant, unprincipled, and so on? Anyone who has followed the fatiguing details of a contemporary academic controversy can easily imagine the possible sources of misunderstanding and their consequences. The interest in the Menger–Schmoller controversy lies in the problems they chose to debate, issues which, for Weber, became the definitive questions of the *Methodenstreit*: the question of the constitutive properties of sociocultural phenomena, the question of the definitive problems of the sociocultural sciences, the question of the essential theoretical purpose or interest of these sciences, and the question of the proper method of sociocultural inquiry. As a methodologist, Weber worked within the parameters established by the Menger–Schmoller debate. The critique of Stammler is one moment in the protracted controversy which began in 1883. By the time Weber enters the *Methodenstreit*, the controversy has been generalized. It transcends the limits of a relatively provincial debate among professional economists. While Menger and Schmoller focus on the logical status of economics, the subject of the controversy between Weber and Stammler is the logical status of the sociocultural sciences in general. Weber's methodological writings deal with each of the four constitutive issues of the *Methodenstreit*, albeit in a piecemeal, unsystematic fashion. The critique of Stammler, however, focuses upon the first: the problem of the definition or constitution of the object of sociocultural knowledge. In order to understand Weber's reasoning in the critique of Stammler, the following are needed. (1) An analysis of the question concerning the definitive features of sociocultural phenomena: this question may be called "the constitutive problem of the sociocultural sciences." (2) An analysis of Weber's solution to this problem: for obvious reasons, this solution may be called "the Verstehen thesis."

The Verstehen Thesis and the Critique of Stammler

What is the subject matter of a sociocultural investigation? What is a sociocultural phenomenon or fact? How are such facts to be identified? This problem is posed in each of Weber's major metatheoretical works. However, it is the critique of Stammler in which Weber provides his most extensive analysis of the import of this problem and its status in a logic of the sociocultural sciences. Weber does not pose the problem by offering a systematic and general account of the conditions under which any item constitutes a possible object of sociocultural inquiry. On the contrary, he raises the problem informally by employing a variety of illustrations.[12] In the critique of Stammler, Weber uses the following illustrations for this purpose: the example of the exchange and the problem of the conditions under which two persons can be identified as performing an act of exchange; the example of the bookmark and the problem of the conditions under which a slip of paper can be identified as a bookmark; the example of Robinson Crusoe and the problem of the conditions under which his conduct can be identified as an attempt to follow an economic maxim; the example of the card game skat, the problem of the conditions under which the three skat players can be described as following the rules of skat, and the problem of the conditions under which any set of proceedings can be identified as a game of skat; and, finally, the example of the legal order and the problem of the conditions under which it can be said that a legal order exists. Consider the predicates that Weber analyzes in the critique of Stammler: exchange, bookmark, economic maxim, the rules of skat, a game of skat, a legal order. The ascription of these predicates putatively identifies some sociocultural "phenomenon"—in the most extensive and permissive sense of this term: some sociocultural datum which, if identified as such, constitutes a possible object of sociocultural investigation. Under what conditions, however, are these predicates truly ascribed to any item? In other words, what are the truth conditions for the ascription of the predicates which identify sociocultural phenomena, the subject matter of sociocultural investigations?

Suppose that we mean by "sociocultural predicate"—or "S-predicate"—not simply any predicate which may be employed in the course of a sociocultural investigation, but rather a predicate of a specific sort: any predicate the ascription of which identifies some item as a sociocultural phenomenon. Then the constitutive problem, the basic issue of the critique of Stammler, may be posed in the following way. What are the peculiarities of S-predicates? What are their essential properties or distinctive features? Since the definitive features of any predicate may be identified by reference to the truth conditions for its ascription, this question can also be articulated in the following way: What are the truth conditions for the ascription of S-predicates? Suppose that we employ this concept of an S-predicate in order to state the constitutive problem. Consider any item x and any S-predicate P. Then the constitutive problem may be identified as the question: Under what conditions is the proposition "Px" true? In other words, what conditions must be satisfied in order for a given S-predicate P to be truly ascribed to a given item x?

Any sociocultural investigation presupposes some answer to this question. Any such inquiry rests upon some method for identifying the object of the inquiry as a sociocultural phenomenon. Put another way, any sociocultural investigation invariably presupposes some answer to the question: What are the truth conditions for the ascription of the

S-predicate that identifies the object of the investigation? This is why Weber calls the solution to the constitutive problem a "transcendental presupposition" of any sociocultural science: it is a logically necessary condition for the possibility of any sociocultural science. So much by way of clarification of the constitutive problem. What is Weber's solution?

According to Weber, there is an essential difference between "meaningful" human conduct—the subject matter of the sociocultural sciences—and "nature." This proposition is perhaps the most fundamental assumption of Weber's methodological work, the axiom on which his other metatheoretical theses rest. He states it for the first time in one of the longest notes of the Roscher essay (Weber, 1975, pp. 217-218). The subject matter of a sociocultural investigation—human action and its artifacts—is already identified or defined as such by the actor himself. Put another way, the contents of any culture are defined or identified as such by the natives who participate in it. At this point, there is a temptation to employ the expression "predefinition" or "predefine," a temptation to which phenomenological social theorists easily succumb. Every sociocultural phenomenon falls under a predefinition. Before the social scientist begins the investigation of an item, it is predefined as a sociocultural phenomenon by the native. From the standpoint of methodology, therefore, the social scientist's task is a peculiar one. He is obliged to investigate phenomena for which an essential and incorrigible account already exists. And what is this account? It is the set of rules, criteria, or principles for the ascription of S-predicates which the natives themselves employ in identifying and distinguishing the phenomena that constitute their sociocultural world. Any society is constituted as such by the native's definitions of its properties. Therefore the initial problem in any sociocultural investigation is to discover how the native ascribes S-predicates. If the investigation is successful, there is a sense in which it should mirror or reproduce the native's own account: the criteria which the social scientist employs for the ascription of a given S-predicate should be equivalent to the criteria which the native employs for the ascription of the same S-predicate.[13]

In articulating this thesis, Weber uses the expressions "meaning" (*"Bedeutung"* or *"Sinn"*),[14] "understanding" (*"Verstehen"*), and "interpretation" (*"Deutung"*). Consider any sociocultural phenomenon. It is identifiable as such only by reference to its meaning, as this meaning is defined or understood by the natives. The ascription of an S-predicate represents an attempt to identify the meaning of some item. It is an attempt to understand or interpret that item. To identify a sociocultural phenomenon is to understand its meaning. Therefore the subject matter of any sociocultural investigation is meaningful, understandable, or interpretable. In Weber's methodology of the sociocultural sciences, these three predicates are truth-functionally equivalent.[15] An item is meaningful if and only if it can be understood or interpreted. The conditions under which an item can be understood are the same as the conditions under which it can be interpreted. To understand the meaning of an item is to interpret it. But what does this mean? In what sense does the ascription of an S-predicate identify an item that is meaningful, interpretable, or understandable?

The ascription of an S-predicate to an item identifies the meaning which the native associates with that item. It follows that there is a sense in which the ascription of an S-predicate represents the native's understanding of his own social life. This might be expressed by saying that there is a sense in which the ascription of an S-predicate must satisfy native criteria for the ascription of this predicate. If the ascription of an S-predicate must satisfy native criteria, then it must be intelligible or understandable to the native himself. In this sense, the item to which the S-predicate is ascribed can be called meaningful: it has a meaning to the native. The ascription of an S-predicate, therefore, constitutes an interpretation: it represents the native's understanding of his own actions and their artifacts. Consider, therefore, some S-predicate P and some item x located in society x. In order to establish that "Px" is true, it is necessary to establish that the natives of S employ a criterion for the ascription of P, a criterion which the proposition "Px" satisfies. Under what conditions is P mistakenly ascribed to x? In order to establish that "Px" is false, it would be sufficient to establish either of the following propositions. The natives of S employ no criterion for the ascription of P. Or, if they apply such a criterion, "Px" does not satisfy it. This is the solution to the constitutive problem which Weber presents in the critique of Stammler.

Suppose we call this solution to the constitutive problem the Verstehen thesis. This is the thesis to which Weber commits the sociocultural sciences in his repeated use of "*Verstehen*" and its cognates. In his view, to identify a sociocultural phenomenon is to identify its meaning as this meaning is understood by the actors or natives. In analyzing the Verstehen thesis, it will be useful to introduce the idea of a Verstehen criterion: the proposition that the ascription of any S-predicate must satisfy native criteria for the ascription of that S-predicate. It will also be useful to introduce the idea of a Verstehen predicate or V-predicate: namely, an S-predicate which is truly ascribed to an item if and only if the Verstehen criterion is satisfied. The Verstehen thesis may then be represented as the claim that all S-predicates are V-predicates. Put another way, the Verstehen thesis is the claim that an S-predicate is truly ascribed if and only if the Verstehen criterion is satisfied.

The Verstehen criterion may be analyzed as follows. The question of whether any S-predicate qualifies as a V-predicate is a question about the conditions under which this predicate is truly ascribed. Consider, therefore, some S-predicate P, some item x, and some society S, the society in which x is located. To say that P is a V-predicate is to say that the assertion "Px" is true if and only if the following proposition is true. There is some criterion C such that: (1) the natives of S employ C as the criterion for the ascription of P, and (2) "Px" satisfies C. This proposition is the Verstehen criterion. Any S-predicate which is truly ascribed to an item if and only if the Verstehen criterion is satisfied is a V-predicate. And any S-predicate the ascription of which is logically independent of either (1) or (2) is not a V-predicate. Therefore the true ascription of any V-predicate to any item turns on the following two considerations. First, do the natives in question employ a criterion for the ascription of this predicate? And, second, does the ascription of the V-predicate to the item x satisfy the native criterion?

This analysis of the Verstehen criterion may be employed to provide a precise statement of the Verstehen thesis. Consider again some S-predicate P, some item x, and some society S, the society in which x is located. The Verstehen thesis is the assertion that "Px" is true if and only if the following proposition is true. There is some criterion C such that: (1) the natives of S employ C as the criterion for the ascription of P, and (2) "Px" satisfies C. The Verstehen thesis claims that the Verstehen criterion is the exclusive test for the ascription of every S-predicate. Therefore the Verstehen thesis entails that the truth conditions for the ascription of V-predicates constitute the truth conditions for the ascription of all S-predicates. This could also be put in the following way: The Verstehen thesis entails that all S-predicates are V-predicates. It follows that anyone who accepts the Verstehen thesis as the solution to the constitutive problem is obliged to treat any question about the identification of sociocultural phenomena as a question concerning the truth conditions for the ascription of some V-predicate. The subject matter of the sociocultural sciences is constituted by all items to which V-predicates may be ascribed. This point could also be stated by defining the concept of a sociocultural phenomenon. A sociocultural phenomenon is any item to which at least one V-predicate can be ascribed. An item to which no V-predicate can be ascribed does not lie within the domain of the sociocultural sciences.

The critique of Stammler contains Weber's most extensive discussion of the Verstehen thesis. The same thesis is sketched in the Roscher-Knies monograph (Weber, 1975, pp. 154, 157-158, 185-186). Here Weber attempts to refute two responses the four constitutive issues of the *Methodenstreit*, a "positivist" response and an "intuitionist" response. His own resolution of these four issues is traced within the context of this critique. The Verstehen thesis is also contained in both the 1904 objectivity essay (Weber, 1968, pp. 170, 175, 177-178, 180-181, 200-201) and the Eduard Meyer monograph (Weber, 1968, p. 262). In these works, however, the constitutive problem is not Weber's principal concern. The Verstehen thesis as developed in the critique of Stammler is stated more clearly—some would say more rigidly—in the famous formulae of the 1913 *Logos* paper and its revision, the prelude to *Economy and Society*. Weber himself notes the intimate relationship between these two papers and the critique of Stammler (Weber, 1968, p. 427, note 1, p. 541). In the critique of Stammler, Weber does not defend the Verstehen thesis by providing an extended argument in its support. Nor does he offer a systematic and general account of the conditions under which any item constitutes a possible object of sociocultural inquiry. On the contrary, the Verstehen thesis is sketched in a number of illustrations and Weber's comments on them: the example of the exchange, the example of the bookmark, the example of Robinson Crusoe, the example of the card game skat, and the example of the legal order. Weber never provides a full account of the points he wants to make in employing these illustrations. His discussion of each example is only a sketch, and the sketch is often blurred by reservations, parenthetical asides, and references to other issues. In some cases, Weber breaks off the discussion of an example after a perfunctory analysis and moves on to other issues. Further, most of these examples are presented in order to illustrate more than one point. Consider, for example, Weber's discussion of the card game skat. He uses this example in order to clarify his solution to the constitutive problem. But he also employs it for several other purposes: to elucidate various senses in which the rules of a game can be called presuppositions; to distinguish axiological, conceptual, and empirical investigations of the properties of rules; to make some critical points against Stammler; and to sketch some theses which will be developed later in his discussion of legal rules. Finally, these illustrations do not seem to be connected by any discussion in which Weber explains the relationship between them. Therefore it should not be surprising that generations of students of Weber's methodological work have found it easy to accept Rickert's judgment: in the critique of Stammler, Weber's reasoning is extraordinarily difficult to follow. Suppose we examine Weber's clearest example, his analysis of the conditions under which two persons can be identified as performing an act of exchange.

> Let us suppose that two men who otherwise engage in no "social relation"—for example, two uncivilized men of different races, or a European who encounters a native in darkest Africa—meet and "exchange" two objects. We are inclined to think that a mere description of what can be observed during this exchange—muscular movements and, if some words were "spoken" the sounds which, so to say, constitute the "material" or "matter" of the behavior—would in no sense comprehend the "essence" of what happens. This is quite correct. The "essence" of what happens is constituted by the "meaning" which the two parties ascribe to their observable behavior, a "meaning" which "regulates" the course of their future conduct. Without this "meaning," we are inclined to say, an "exchange" is neither empirically possible nor conceptually imaginable (Weber, below, p. 109).

Under what conditions does an instance of observed behavior qualify as an exchange? Under what conditions is it true to say that behavior constitutes an exchange? In other words, what are the truth conditions for the ascription of the S-predicate "exchange"? Consider the instructive example of Malinowski's pioneering ethnographical work. Suppose we join him on that first anthropologically fateful journey to New Guinea. It is March, 1915. While pursuing his studies in the northern Massim, Malinowski casually noticed one of his informants offering a heavy necklace of red shell disks to a friend (Malinowski, 1967, p. 94). Although he did not realize it at the time, this was a *soulava*, one of the two artifacts of central importance to that complex of exchanges Malinowski later called "the Kula." This was apparently Malinowski's first "observation" of the Kula. In view of the significance of his later studies of this institution, it was a remarkably inauspicious beginning. In March, 1915, as his diary clearly indicates, Malinowski did not know that the presentation of the necklace was part of the celebrated Kula exchange. Indeed, at that particular point, he was not prepared to identify what he saw as part of any exchange. He was not prepared to ascribe any S-predicate to it. During the following two years of work in the Trobriand Islands, what happened that led Malinowski to identify the presentation of the necklace as an act essentially different from and much more complex than the offering of a gift? Under what conditions would Malinowski be justified in identifying the presentation of the necklace as part of the Kula exchange? Put another way, what are the truth conditions for the ascription of the S-predicate "Kula exchange"?

Weber's answer runs as follows. The behavior in question constitutes an instance of the Kula exchange if and only if the actors themselves ascribe this meaning to their conduct. The same point can also be articulated in the language Weber later favors in his 1913 *Logos* paper. Behavior qualifies as part of the Kula exchange if and only if the actors themselves associate this "subjective meaning" with their conduct, if and only if their behavior can be interpreted or understood as part of the Kula exchange. The same point can be stated in the language employed in the above analysis of the Verstehen thesis. Malinowski would be justified in identifying what he saw as an instance of the Kula exchange only if the natives themselves employ a criterion for the ascription of the predicate "Kula exchange." Further, the behavior Malinowski observed must also satisfy this native criterion. If the natives employ no criterion for the ascription of the predicate "Kula exchange," then no instance of their behavior can be identified as a case of such an exchange. And if the behavior observed by Malinowski fails to satisfy the native criterion, then it does not qualify as part of the Kula exchange. Consider, therefore, some behavior x of two Trobrianders and the S-predicate "Kula exchange." The behavior x can be identified as an instance of the Kula exchange if and only if there is some criterion C such that: (1) the Trobrianders themselves employ C as the criterion for the ascription of the predicate "Kula exchange," and (2) the ascription of the predicate "Kula exchange" to the behavior x satisfies C. In other words, the predicate "Kula exchange" can be ascribed to the conduct Malinowski observed if and only if the Verstehen criterion is satisfied.

As Weber puts it, independent of the "meaning" the actors ascribe to their conduct, an exchange is "neither empirically possible nor conceptually imaginable." It is difficult to determine exactly what Weber means by this language. Perhaps the following approximates an account of his intentions. Suppose that the actors employ no criterion for the ascription of the S-predicate "exchange." Suppose that they never ascribe this meaning to their conduct because they have no concept of an exchange. In that case, it would not make sense to describe any act they perform as an exchange. The reason: To describe their conduct as an exchange implies that they employ a criterion for the the ascription of the predicate "exchange." But that is, *ex hypothesi,* not the case. Under these conditions, as Weber says, an exchange would not be conceptually imaginable. Suppose, on the other hand, that the actors employ a criterion for the ascription of the predicate "exchange." But suppose that the behavior observed by the social scientist does not satisfy this criterion. Or, as Weber would say, suppose that it does not have this meaning. In this case—although it is "conceptually imaginable" that the actors might perform an act of exchange since they employ a criterion for the ascription of this predicate—the description of their behavior as an act of exchange would, in fact, be false. Or, as Weber puts it, in this case an exchange would not be "empirically possible." This is because the actors do not in fact ascribe this meaning to their conduct. Because the native criterion for the ascription of the predicate "exchange" is not satisfied, their conduct would be empirically inexplicable—or, as Weber sometimes says, causally inexplicable—as an exchange. Reconsider the Trobrianders. Suppose that they do not ascribe the predicate "Kula exchange" to the conduct Malinowski observed. This would be a consequence of either of the two following possibilities. The first: The Trobrianders employ no criterion for the ascription of this predicate. This might be expressed by saying that they have no concept of a Kula exchange. Therefore no instance of their behavior can be identified as a case of this sociocultural phenomenon. This is because their conduct is not even "conceptually imaginable" as a Kula exchange. The second possibility: Although the Trobrianders employ a criterion for the ascription of the predicate "Kula exchange," the behavior observed by Malinowski does not satisfy this criterion. Although the Trobrianders may engage in Kula exchanges, what Malinowski observed does not qualify as one of these exchanges. It follows that it is not in fact possible to identify this behavior as an instance of the Kula exchange. In both cases, according to Weber, the predicate "Kula exchange" cannot be ascribed to the behavior Malinowski observed. This is because the condition for the ascription of this predicate—the requirement that the actors identify their own conduct as an instance of the Kula exchange—is not satisfied. In other words, the Verstehen criterion states the truth conditions for the ascription of this S-predicate.

The foregoing analysis of the truth conditions for the ascription of the S-predicate "exchange," according to Weber, applies to all S-predicates. The Verstehen criterion states the truth conditions for the ascription of every S-predicate. The other illustrations Weber employs in the critique of Stammler confirm this claim. Consider, for example, the bookmark illustration. Under what conditions does a slip of paper that I place between the pages of a book qualify as a bookmark? Only if I ascribe this meaning to the slip of paper, only if I mean or intend to use it as a bookmark. Weber's point in this example may be articulated as follows. Consider a slip of paper x which I place between the pages of a book and the predicate "bookmark." The slip of paper x can be identified as a bookmark if and only if there is some criterion C such that: (1) I employ C as the criterion for the ascription of the predicate "bookmark," and (2) the slip of paper x satisfies C. Unless the Verstehen criterion is satisfied—or, as Weber puts it, "independent of the knowledge of this meaning," the meaning which the slip of paper has for the actor— the act of placing the slip of paper between the pages of a book "would remain causally inexplicable." Apparently this is Weber's way of expressing the following point. Suppose that a social scientist observes a native placing a slip of paper between the pages of a book. And suppose that he does not know whether the native employs a criterion for the ascription of the predicate "bookmark." Or suppose that, although he knows that the native employs this criterion, he does not know whether the behavior he observes satisfies that criterion. In either of these two cases, what he observes remains "casually inexplicable." He is unable to explain what the native is doing or why he is doing it because he is unable to identify what the native is doing. He cannot identify what the native is doing because—to use Weber's language—he is unable to discover the meaning which the native associates with his conduct. Or, to use the language of this essay, he is unable to discover the predicate which the native ascribes to his own conduct. Which is to say: Unless the observer can discover an S-predicate that the native ascribes to his own conduct, he cannot determine what the native is doing. Weber illustrates the same thesis in his discussion of the game of skat. What does it mean to say that the three skat players follow the rules of skat? Under what conditions can three persons be identified as playing a game of skat? Only under the following conditions. There is some criterion C, the rules or the "normative maxims" of the game, such that: (1) the three players employ C as the criterion for the ascription of the predicate "game of skat," and (2) their own conduct satisfies C—in other words, they follow the rules of the game.[16]

Are these illustrations trivial and uninteresting, perhaps excessively so? The reader who takes this view might consider the following. All of the "basic concepts of interpretive sociology" that Weber analyzes at the beginning of *Economy and Society* are constituted in exactly the same fashion. They are all S-predicates which are truly ascribed if and only if the Verstehen criterion is satisfied. What holds for the relatively simple predicates "bookmark" and "game of skat" also holds for the concept of a social relation, the types of social action, the concept of a legitimate order, and the other complex and sociologically fundamental predicates which provide the conceptual framework for *Economy and Society*: the Verstehen criterion states the truth conditions for the ascription of the constitutive concepts or the basic S-predicates of "interpretive sociology."

Weber, of course, also takes the following possibility into account. The social scientist may ascribe some meaning to the proceedings he observes even though he does not know whether the native ascribes this meaning to his own conduct. In other words, he may ascribe some S-predicate to some putative sociocultural phenomenon even though he does not know whether the native ascribes the same S-predicate to the same phenomenon, even though he does not know whether the Verstehen criterion is satisfied. Suppose we examine this possibility and reconsider the predicament of Malinowski in his attempt to identify the essential features of the Kula exchange. He might ascribe some hypothetical meaning to an apparent exchange he observes. To employ Weber's language, he might ask:

Following the observed completion of the act of exchanging the objects, how "must" the two "exchange partners" behave if their conduct is to correspond to the "idea" of the exchange? In other words, suppose that their subsequent conduct conformed to the logical consequences of the "meaning" which *we* ascribe to their conduct. If this were the case, how would they have to behave? Therefore we begin with the following empirical fact. Processes of a certain sort have *in fact* taken place. A certain "meaning" is ideationally associated with these processes. It is not a "meaning" which has been analyzed clearly and distinctly, but rather a "meaning" which is only vaguely associated with these processes. Then, however, we *abandon* the domain of the empirical and pose the following question: How must the "meaning" of the conduct of the actors be conceptually construed in order to produce an internally consistent conceptual construct of that "meaning"? In other words, we are engaged in what could be called a dogmatics" of "meaning" (Weber, below, pp. 111-112).

This "dogmatic" conceptual construct of the meaning of the exchange, Weber says, may prove to be very useful as an "heuristic principle for framing hypotheses." These hypotheses would provide putative answers to the question: What S-predicates may be ascribed to the behavior in question? However, Malinowski's ascription of some predicate to the conduct of the Trobrianders—this is what Weber calls a dogmatic conceptual construct—is only an hypothesis. Under what conditions can this hypothesis be verified? Only by resolving the following question. Consider Malinowski's dogmatic conceptual construct and the meaning it ascribes to the conduct of the Trobrianders. Is this also the meaning that the actors themselves associate with their conduct? This question may also be posed in the following way. Are the S-predicates that Malinowski ascribes to the conduct of the Trobrianders also among the S-predicates which they ascribe to their own conduct? In order to establish that his dogmatic conceptual construct actually identifies some sociocultural phenomenon, therefore, Malinowski is obliged to resolve the following problem. Does this conceptual construct—his ascription of an S-predicate to the conduct of the Trobrianders—satisfy the Verstehen criterion? If the Verstehen criterion is satisfied, then he has succeeded in identifying a sociocultural phenomenon. If the Verstehen criterion is not satisfied, then he has not succeeded. This is the Verstehen thesis, the solution to the constitutive problem that Weber offers in the critique of Stammler.[17]

Weber's critique of Stammler is caustic, brutal, and unqualified by the reservations he often introduces on behalf of other writers he criticizes. Later, in the revision of the 1913 *Logos* paper published in *Economy and Society*, Weber introduces an equivocal note of apology, explaining that the severity of his essay was a response to Stammler's many errors (Weber, 1968, p. 575, note 1). Stammler, we learn, is a bad writer and a shoddy thinker. In spite of the "extravagant pretensions" of the book and Stammler's "staggering confidence," his prose is vague, ambiguous, and "slovenly." In consequence, Stammler repeatedly confuses both his reader and himself. He is accused of "the most intolerable obscurities and contradictions imaginable." Weber describes the result as a thicket of apparent truths, half truths, truths incorrectly formulated, covert falsities, scholastic fallacies, and sophisms. This last remark articulates a more serious objection. The vagueness, ambiguity, and obscurity of Stammler's style seems to be intentional. Weber represents Stammler's style of imprecision as a technique of subterfuge and equivocation. Its purpose is to mystify the reader. Stammler, in short, is accused of sophistry and intellectual dishonesty. Curiously, Weber emphatically denies that this is a "moral" criticism of Stammler and his work. Yet he also claims that Stammler's book is "exhaustively and exclusively based upon" sophisms, and Stammler himself, we are told, is "totally irresponsible" in his disregard of the intellectual obligations of the serious scholarly writer.

Although Weber criticizes Stammler on many grounds, his main objections are concerned with Stammler's misconception of the constitutive problem.[18] The purpose of the critique of Stammler could be described in the following way. Weber attempts to defend his conception of an interpretive sociocultural science—a sociocultural science committed to the Verstehen thesis—by examining the logical properties of one of its provinces, the sociology of law. Weber supports his view of an interpretive sociology of law polemically by comparing it with Stammler's "teleological" conception. According to Weber, legal norms are identifiable and causally explicable only if subjective meaning can be ascribed to them, only if they fall under an interpretation. Or, in the language of the foregoing analysis, the predicate "legal norm" can be ascribed to an item if and only if the ascription of that predicate to this item satisfies the Verstehen criterion. "Legal norm," in other words, is a Verstehen predicate. Weber wants to show that subjective meanings—"ideas in the mind of a judge," for example—constitute the basis of the empirical regularity of a legal norm. Only an interpretive sociology of law, a sociology which is committed to the Verstehen thesis—the necessity of identifying the subjective meaning which the actors in a system of legal norms intend—can explain why this regularity obtains. As Weber interprets it, the purpose of Stammler's book is also to resolve the constitutive problem. But the solution which Stammler offers is a failure. In the critique—which varies from a clinically detached dissection of Stammler's reasoning to impatient, sarcastic, and contemptuous remarks on Stammler's scientific and scholarly personality—Weber analyzes the sources of Stammler's confusion: his conflation of axiological and nonaxiological questions; his failure to distinguish empirical problems from logical and epistemological problems; and, closely related to these two sources of confusion, Stammler's "scholasticism"—his assumption that the substantive problems of an empirical science can be resolved by logical, conceptual, or epistemological analysis. In a first reading, however, these criticisms and their bearing upon Weber's attempt to sketch his own solution to the constitutive problem are not easy to follow. As Weber once said of his discussion of Knies, he seems to use Stammler as a pretext for the presentation of his own views on methodological issues. According to Marianne, Weber's view of the methodological writer's obligations to his reader is expressed in the maxim: Let the reader take the same pains as the writer himself. A severe doctrine. However the patient and diligent reader who has the capacity for this austere discipline—a variety of Weberian ascetic self-resignation—will learn that Weber applied it in the critique of Stammler.

Notes

1. On the basis of this account of the constitutive property of social life, Stammler concludes that human society is the domain of purposive behavior. Purposive behavior falls under teleological explanations. It is to be distinguished from the domain of nature, which falls under causal explanations. See the section of Weber's critique entitled: "Causality and Teleology" in Stammler's Work. Stammler's distinction between nature and society seems to be a variation upon Kant's distinction between the kingdom of necessity—nature—and the kingdom of freedom—human action. It is, in fact, the convention in the history and philosophy of law to classify Stammler as a neo-Kantian, the most prominent neo-Kantian legal scholar of his time. See, for example, Friedrich,

1963, pp. 157, 163*n*. 13. As we shall see, Weber rejects this view of Stammler's work. According to Weber, Stammler's profession that his philosophy of the sociocultural sciences is grounded upon Kant's theory of knowledge is merely an empty and disingenuous pretension. Herman Kantorowicz—who describes Weber's critique as a "brilliant essay"—supports Weber's contention. The aims of Stammler's book, he claims, are unattainable, its methods are useless, and its concepts are either unclear or sterile (see Kantorowicz, 1909, p. 10). The question of the real meaning of Stammler's text is complicated by the imprecision and obscurity of his prose, the object of repeated and mercilessly caustic objections by Weber. For a much more sympathetic view of Stammler's work and his status as a neo-Kantian, see Larenz, 1931, pp. 10–17, 76–81. See also Larenz, 1960, pp. 83–92 and especially p. 91*n*. 1, where Larenz argues that Weber is guilty of a "grandiose misunderstanding" of Stammler's book.

2. The *Archiv* is now regarded as one of the most distinguished scholarly journals in the history of the sociocultural sciences. In 1903, Weber, Edgar Jaffé, and Werner Sombart assumed a joint editorship. Jaffé was also a Heidelberg economist and the husband of Weber's student and close friend Else von Richthofen. Sombart, one year younger than Weber, is sufficiently well known as another brilliant student of the origins of modern capitalism. During their joint editorship, the *Archiv* published work of extraordinarily high quality. Between 1904 and 1909, essays by Michels, Radbruch, Simmel, Sombart, Spann, Tönnies, Troeltsch, and several contributions by Weber himself all appeared in the *Archiv*. Much of the work for which Weber is now remembered—including the entire series of studies in the sociology of religion, from *The Protestant Ethic and the Spirit of Capitalism* to *Ancient Judaism*—originally appeared as monographs in the *Archiv*.

3. Therefore it is difficult to resist the conclusion that Weber's metatheoretical works are fragmentary, unfinished, and programmatic. Weber himself would not contest this judgment. From his perspective of the methodology of the sociocultural sciences, however, this is not a defect peculiar to Weber's own work. It is not a defect of any sort. According to Weber, the construction of a definitive and exhaustive system of concepts is not a possible theoretical goal of the sociocultural sciences. Weber conceives reality as an endless

"stream" of events. Reality is both extensively and intensively infinite. Because it is endless, a complete description of the entire stream is impossible. An exhaustive description of any single phenomenon within this stream is also impossible. This is because reality is subject to an infinite number and variety of variations. It is in a state of perpetual flux. The sociocultural sciences, therefore, focus only upon selected aspects of phenomena: those to which "cultural meaning" can be ascribed. The subject matter of the sociocultural sciences is the domain of cultural meanings. The contents of this domain, however, are not invariable either. Since it is part of the endless and perpetual flux of reality, the domain of cultural meanings is also subject to variations and transformations. What follows?

> The conceptual frameworks within which the social world can be an object of observation and scientific explanation are impermanent. The presuppositions of the sociocultural sciences remain variable into the indefinite future, at least as long as an Oriental petrification of thought does not stultify the capacity to raise new questions about the inexhaustible nature of social life (Weber, 1968, p. 184).

Consider the "presuppositions" of the sociocultural sciences, the "conceptual frameworks" within which a science of the sociocultural is possible. In other words, consider the premises of any sociocultural methodology. Like the subject matter of the sociocultural sciences—"cultural meanings" and their transformations— these premises are also impermanent, perpetually subject to revision, variation, and rejection. It follows that any sociocultural methodology is essentially incomplete. Put another way, incompleteness is a logical property of methodology within the domain of the sociocultural. Any such methodology is necessarily fragmentary and unfinished, only one among an indefinite number of other possible programs for sociocultural research. It follows that the sociocultural disciplines are among those sciences that are "endowed with eternal youth." This is because "culture in its endless progressions invariably leads these disciplines to novel problematics" (Weber, 1968, p. 206). From Weber's perspective, therefore, the belief that any metatheoretical work in the sociocultural sciences could or should provide a finished and conclusive solution to any set of methodological problems is an illusion.

4. *Collected Essays on the Philosophy of Science.* "*Wissenschaftslehre*" might also be translated as "theory of science"—a theory which is *about* science, a theory which takes scientific inquiry as its subject matter—or as "metascience." The word "*Wissenschaftslehre*" does not appear in any of the essays contained in the *Wissenschaftslehre*. Nor is there any reason to believe that Weber himself would have collected these various essays and monographs—published over a period of more than fifteen years, composed under very different circumstances, and written for a variety of purposes—into a single volume. We owe both the volume and the word to Marianne. Why did she choose this title? After all, it seems to promise much: that Weber had worked out a philosophy of science which these essays contain. But there are other possibilities. Perhaps she only wanted to identify the problems which the essays raise: they are concerned with questions that arise in the philosophy of science. Perhaps she was influenced by her own research on Fichte (Marianne Weber, 1900). He wrote a book entitled *Grundlage der gesamten Wissenschaftslehre* (1794): roughly, *The Foundations of a Complete Philosophy of Science*. Perhaps she was influenced by her philosophical studies with Heinrich Rickert: Weber's contemporary, colleague at Freiburg, friend of the family, and—as at least some commentators, including Rickert himself, judge—Weber's principal philosophical mentor. In *The Limits of Concept Formation in the Natural Sciences* (1902), a book Weber repeatedly cites as influencing the development of his own methodological views, Rickert describes his inquiry as *Wissenschaftslehre* or *Methodologie*, in order to distinguish it from both metaphysics and epistemology (see Rickert, 1902, pp. 10–15, 22, 156n., 215n., 601–602). Is Weber's methodology a species of Rickertian *Wissenschaftslehre*?

These unresolved possibilities are a matter of considerable controversy. Did Weber try to work out a philosophy of science, or at least a philosophy of sociocultural science? Or can a coherent philosophy of science be identified in his methodological essays, even though the development of such a philosophy was not Weber's intention? Did Weber develop a philosophy of science which remained imperfect or flawed: incomplete, ungrounded, or erroneous in certain details? Or did Weber limit himself to the resolution of a few methodological problems posed by the development of the sociocultural sciences in Germany? Was Weber a philosopher of science? Or was he simply a professional social scientist who, given the problematical state of his discipline, found himself obliged to deal with certain methodological issues? There are, of course, other possibilities. The extreme polar positions in this debate seem to be represented by Henrich and Tenbruck, both authors of valuable studies on the *Wissenschaftslehre*. According to Henrich, the essays in the *Wissenschaftslehre* "are not merely preliminary contributions to the development of a possible future philosophy of science. On the contrary, they already constitute a complete philosophy of science" (Henrich, 1952, p. 2). According to Tenbruck, the essays in the *Wissenschaftslehre* do not contain a philosophy of science. Nor was their purpose the presentation of a philosophy of science. Weber's only intention in writing these essays was to solve certain problems in the "logic of the sociocultural sciences"—problems posed by the contemporary predicament of the disciplines in which Weber himself worked (see Tenbruck, 1959, pp. 574, 576, 582, 583, 613, 625). Like many of the debates on the *Wissenschaftslehre*, this one concerns basic concepts which remain unclarified and crucial distinctions which remain problematical. In order to resolve this controversy, it is necessary to discover how Weber conceived the differences between philosophy (metaphysics and epistemology), logic (metatheory or methodology), and substantive sociocultural theory. Curiously, Runciman ignores all these issues in his essay on the *Wissenschaftslehre*. He assumes that Weber's essays contain a coherent philosophy of science and then proceeds to criticize the philosophical positions he attributes to Weber (Runciman, 1972, pp. 8-9).

In this controversy, the question of the relationship between Rickert's philosophy of science and Weber's methodology is especially difficult to assess. Is there some sense in which Weber was Rickert's disciple? Was Rickert his "philosophical master" (see Hughes, 1958, p. 309)? On the preponderance of Rickert's influence, see also Rickert (1926 and 1929) and von Schelting (1934). Weber's many references to Rickert might suggest this. He never cites any of his other contemporaries so often or so approvingly. Or were these citations simply a magnanimous gesture to a former colleague and a family friend? The original parties to this dispute seem to have been Rickert himself and Karl Jaspers. Jaspers became acquainted with Weber in 1909. The following is his view of the relationship between Weber and Rickert. Weber noticed that some of the methodological positions he had developed independently were also contained in Rickert's 1902 treatise. Weber, "extravagantly and nobly unselfish" when it came to matters of this sort, cited Rickert in his essays whenever these logical problems were at issue. The misleading result: "some of his discussions merely seem to be logical consequences and applications of Rickert's ideas" (Jasper's, 1958b, p. 310). Jaspers also reports on a conversation he had with Rickert in Heidelberg five days after Weber's death. Rickert "had begun to speak of Weber as his pupil" and referred to the "limited significance and influence" of Weber's work. Jaspers' reply: "Do you mean that anyone at all will read you in the future? If that happens, it will only be due to the fact that you are mentioned in the notes of Weber's works as someone to whom he owes certain logical insights" (Jaspers, 1958b, p. 311). "After that," Jaspers laconically adds, "relations between Rickert and myself became strained." In retrospect, Jaspers' judgment on the fate of Rickert's philosophy does not seem to have been too severe. Shortly after Weber's death, Jaspers was asked to read a memorial address on Weber to the Heidelberg students. This occurred on July 17, 1920 (see Jaspers, 1926). Rickert, according to Jaspers, offered the following response to the address. "Of course you can make a philosophy out of Max Weber if you want to. But to call him a philosopher? That is absurd" (Jaspers, 1958b, p. 311). On Jaspers' view of Weber as a philosopher, see also Jaspers, 1958a. The entire complex historical question of the relationship between Weber and his predecessors or precursors remains obscure. Excellent suggestions are contained in Tenbruck's 1959 paper, but very little has been done to follow them up. Exceptions are the recent works of Loos (1970), Bruun (1972), and Burger (1976). In order to resolve the problem of the genesis of Max Weber's methodology, special monographs on the following relationships are obviously needed: Weber and the Historical School of economics in Germany, Weber and the various forms of naturalistic historiography—

evolutionary, Marxist, positivist—that were fashionable in his time, Weber and Menger, Weber and Dilthey, Weber and Rickert, and Weber and Simmel.

5. Edward Shils has translated some of the best examples of Weber's polemical prose (Weber, 1974). See especially "The Alleged 'Academic Freedom' of the German Universities" and "The Academic Freedom of the Universities." Shils' translations of these pieces, perhaps intentionally, are somewhat wooden. They do not recapture the caustic irony and the contemptuous sarcasm of the original.

6. The principal questions analyzed here and in the next section of this essay are considered from another perspective in Oakes, 1977.

7. See Weber, 1968, p. 215. Weber's remarks at the beginning of the Eduard Meyer monograph have led Tenbruck to conclude that Weber conceived his own methodological work in the same way (Tenbruck, 1959, p. 582). Tenbruck's thesis may be stated as follows. In one sense, Weber is a methodologist: he diagnoses the various diseases that have infected the sociocultural sciences. In another sense, however, he is not: Weber fails to provide a cure. In Tenbruck's view, Weber describes the definitive issues of the *Methodenstreit*. But he does not attempt to resolve them. This view of Weber's methodology seems to be mistaken. Weber the methodologist is not comparable to a patient describing his symptoms to a specialist. He is comparable to the physician who attempts to heal himself and anyone else who suffers from the same disease. Tenbruck's mistake on this point—if it is a mistake—is a consequence of his view of the crucial significance of Weber's programmatic 1904 essay on objectivity. This view of the 1904 essay is shared by many students of Weber's methodology, and it is one of the very few issues on which Tenbruck and Henrich agree. In the 1904 essay, Weber the methodologist is indeed comparable to the patient describing his symptoms. Weber makes this quite clear in his introduction to the essay. His only purpose is to point out problems, not to offer solutions (Weber, 1968, pp. 146*n.*, 148, 205). In other words, Weber sees the essay on objectivity in the same way that he sees Eduard Meyer's epistemological reflections: a patient's description of his symptoms, but not a cure. However, this is not the methodological problematic of the Roscher–Knies

monograph, the Eduard Meyer monograph, or the critique of Stammler. In these works, Weber is not merely describing symptoms or reporting on the *Methodenstreit*. He is prescribing a cure or attempting to resolve some of the constitutive issues of the *Methodenstreit*. Yet to Tenbruck, the essay on objectivity represents the "genuine breakthrough" in Weber's methodology (Tenbruck, 1959, p. 612). It is not simply another version of the ideas Weber had already developed in the Roscher-Knies monograph. On the contrary, it represents a new stage in Weber's methodological development. It is the definitive statement of Weber's methodology. Weber's later methodological work is simply an attempt to test, expand, and complete the insights already contained in the 1904 essay (see Tenbruck, 1959, pp. 579, 611). This view of the crucial status of the essay on objectivity also seems to be mistaken (on these points, see the "Introductory Essay" to Weber, 1975, and Oakes, 1977).

8. If this account of Weber's perception of the sociocultural sciences is sound, then the bearing of Kuhn's analysis of scientific change upon Weber's situation is obvious (see Kuhn, 1970). Confronted by the conflict of paradigms and the impossibility of doing normal science—the sort of science that Weber did from the time of his graduate work to the time of his "breakdown"—Weber finds himself in a revolutionary predicament. His response to this crisis is the response of the revolutionary scientist: he begins to formulate the elements of a new paradigm. In various unconnected passages scattered throughout his methodological essays (see, for example, Weber, 1968, pp. 147-148, 160-161, 214, 218, and also the lecture "Science as a Vocation"), Weber seems to have anticipated Kuhn's theses concerning the relationship between paradigms or problematics, normal science, and revolutionary science. There is a temptation to conclude that Weber conceived his methodology as comparable to the methodological work of other revolutionary scientists. Rickert yields to this temptation (Rickert, 1926, p. 228).

9. This is not a complete account of Weber's view of the uses of methodology in the sociocultural sciences. He also claims that it can be valuable for two other purposes. (a) The social scientist who is methodologically sophisticated "can never be impressed by a philosophically embellished dilettantism" (Weber, 1968, p. 217).

Methodology sharpens the critical faculties. It eliminates philosophical naïveté and provides a useful tool for the destruction of idols of the theater. This is one of the purposes of Weber's critique of Stammler. Stammler's book, in Weber's view, is a good example of what he calls a "philosophically embellished dilettantism." (b) Any conceptual scheme is necessarily limited—or, as Weber often puts it, one-sided. It focuses only on certain aspects of reality. It implies that some questions are important, significant, or crucial, and it excludes other questions as unimportant, uninteresting, or irrelevant. It only legitimates the use of certain kinds of methods and theories. Methodology is useful when it exposes these limitations. By comparing the assumptions of one conceptual scheme with other possibilities, methodology functions as a "critique of concept formation and conceptual schemes" (Weber, 1968, pp. 206-207).

10. Such an analysis would include a reconsideration of the following piece of scholarly wisdom. German sociocultural science is to be understood as an idealist, romanticist, historicist reaction to the rationalist, materialist, ahistorical sociocultural thought of Western Europe—especially France and England—during the seventeenth and eighteenth centuries. A good exposition of this view, provided by a scholar who was apprently among those responsible for creating it, is contained in Ernst Troeltsch's book *Deutscher Geist und Westeuropa* (1925). According to Troeltsch, elements of this antirationalist tradition, a tradition that he regards as peculiarly German, can be traced back to Luther, even to Meister Eckhart (see also Troeltsch, 1922). For a recent vulgarization of this thesis, see Gouldner's "Romanticism and Classicism: Deep Structures in Social Science" (1973). Gouldner attempts to incorporate Weber into a "Romantic" tradition of sociocultural thought. "Weber's focus," according to Gouldner, is "typically Romantic both in its ultimate objective as well as in its methodology" (Gouldner, 1973, p. 341). We also learn that the "Weberian conception of social science" entails "a systematic application of Romantic premises" (Gouldner, 1973, p. 342). This is a typical misconception of Weber's methodological work (see the "Introductory Essay" to Weber, 1975). There is useful material on Weber and the *Methodenstreit* in Tenbruck (1959), Loos (1970), and Bruun (1972). On the development of the *Methodenstreit* within the *Verein für*

Sozialpolitik, see Lindenlaub (1967). For a more general picture of the *Methodenstreit* as one element of a pervasive crisis of Western civilization, see Ringer (1969). Mitzman (1973) thinks that this generalized cultural crisis was an important influence on the work of Weber and his contemporaries. In this study, Mitzman concentrates on Tönnies, Sombart, and Michels.

11. Menger replied to Schmoller's review in 1884 with a small book entitled *The Errors of Historicism in German Economics*. The book is written as a parady of a style favored during the seventeenth and eighteenth centuries. It is a collection of sixteen letters addressed to a sympathetic patron. The temper of the book fully justifies Weber's characterization: it is "Menger's furious response" to Schmoller's review (Weber, 1975, p. 94). It is difficult to see how Schmoller could have taken Menger's work of 1883 "personally." Although the book is a critique of the Historical School, Schmoller himself is only mentioned twice. He is given a favorable citation in a footnote (Menger, 1883, p. 279n. 153), and he is mentioned among the followers of Knies, surely, from Schmoller's perspective, an unobjectionable reference (Menger, 1883, p. 230). In the letters of 1884, however, the level of the controversy deteriorates considerably. The dispute is no longer restricted to the domain, problems, purposes, and methods of economics or the sociocultural sciences in general. Moral and political considerations enter the debate. In addition to the conflicting claims of two alternative sociocultural problematics, the merits of Schmoller and Menger, Berlin and Vienna, Prussia and Austria are at issue. If Menger's 1883 book is a critique of the German Historical School, the 1884 letters are a critique of Schmoller and what, in Menger's view, he represents. We learn that Schmoller is guilty of "the crudest misunderstandings" (Menger, 1884, p. 4). As a polemicist, he is "ruthless in his choice of weapons," the "master of a style of writing that is as vulgar as it is personal—the only kind of virtuosity that can be ascribed to his prose style" (Menger, 1884, p. 6). As an editor, Schmoller is "irresponsible" (Menger, 1884, p. 10). As a methodologist, he is lacking in "the most elementary and basic knowledge of questions concerning scientific methodology." Schmoller "continually confuses the simplest metatheoretical concepts" (Menger, 1884, p. 72). The logic of this controversy is representative of the *Methodenstreit* as it developed in the three decades before World War I.

Disputes which were originally methodological are transformed into controversies over personalities and the alleged political and ethical consequences of alternative methodologies. In September, 1914, as is well known, German methodologists of the sociocultural sciences acquired a new preoccupation which eclipsed the *Methodenstreit:* the "ideas of 1914." For more details on the Menger-Schmoller dispute and the *Methodenstreit* in German economics, see Brinkmann (1950) and Ritzel (1950).

12. This is also the status of the constitutive problem in Weber's earlier metatheoretical works. Weber poses the constitutive problem by considering examples of the conditions under which an item may be identified as a specific kind of sociocultural phenomenon. In the Roscher-Knies monograph, Weber raises the following questions for this purpose. Under what conditions does a disease—Weber considers syphilis and the bubonic plague—qualify as a cultural phenomenon? Under what conditions does a disease constitute a sociocultural fact (Weber, 1975, pp. 141, 157)? Under what conditions can a given text be identified as a military command (Weber, 1975, p. 154)? Under what conditions can the policies of Friedrich Wilhelm IV be identified (Weber, 1975, p. 189)? In the objectivity essay, Weber raises the following questions for the same purpose. Under what conditions can "cultural meaning" be ascribed to a given fact—for example, exchange, the money economy, religion, and prostitution (Weber, 1968, pp. 176, 177, 181)? In the monograph on Eduard Meyer, Weber poses the constitutive problem by considering the conditions under which the "cultural" or "historical meaning" of a given object (*Faust*, for example) can be "interpreted" (Weber, 1968, p. 262).

13. There is also, according to Weber, an important sense in which the sociocultural investigation does not reproduce the native's account. It does not qualify as the expression of a unique kind of "intuition" that can be achieved only within the sociocultural sciences—a "recreation" or "reproduction" of the "immediate experience" embodied in some sociocultural phenomenon (Weber, 1975, p. 169). Nor does it express a diffuse, unanalyzable feeling which is the result of the investigator's gift for "sympathetic" or "empathetic" participation in the actions of others (Weber, 1975, pp. 177–178). The ascription of an S-predicate does not express a feeling of any sort. In other words, Weber emphatically rejects

what might be called an intuitionist solution to the constitutive problem. Therefore it is surprising that much of the Anglo-American literature on Weber's methodology attributes an intuitionist solution to him, a position which he explicitly rejects and attempts to refute. See, for example, Abel (1948), Martindale (1959), Popper (1963), Wrong (1970), Leat (1972), and Gouldner (1973).

14. In the Roscher–Knies monograph, the 1904 objectivity essay, the Eduard Meyer monograph, and the critique of Stammler, Weber uses *"Bedeutung"*—which can also mean "importance" or "significance"—more often than *"Sinn."* Further, He uses "Bedeutung" in several different senses: (a) to refer to the meaning that the native ascribes to a sociocultural phenomenon (Weber, 1968, p. 332); (b) to refer to the meaning that "we"—the social scientists—ascribe to a sociocultural phenomenon (Weber, 1968, pp. 175–176); (c) to refer to the importance or significance—for example, the "world-historical" importance or significance—that the social scientists who are the bearers of the values of Western civilization ascribe to a sociocultural phenomenon (Weber, 1968, p. 153). There are contexts in which it is very difficult to determine which of these three senses Weber intends. Unfortunately these are among the most crucial and potentially illuminating passages in Weber's methodological work (see, for example, Weber, 1968, pp. 170, 177–178, 180–181, 184–185, 213–214). In his 1913 *Logos* essay and also in the revision of this essay which he placed at the beginning of *Economy and Society*, *"Bedeutung"* disappears almost completely and is replaced by *"Sinn."* The above ambiguity also disappears. In these two writings, *"Sinn"* refers to the meaning—which Weber often calls "subjective meaning"—that the native or actor ascribes to his actions and their artifacts. In the *Logos* paper, Weber uses *"Bedeutung"* only twice. In both instances, *"Bedeutung"* refers to changes or transformations of meaning: *"Bedeutungswandel"* (Weber, pp. 449, 472). In the revision of this paper for *Economy and Society*, he uses *"Bedeutung"* once, in the unambiguous sense of historical importance or significance (Weber, 1968, p. 545).

15. The phrase "in Weber's methodology of the sociocultural sciences" should be stressed. Weber's methodological writings contain the outlines of a more general theory of interpretation. His theory of sociocultural interpretation is only one component of this more comprehensive theory. According to Weber, there are varieties of

interpretation which are irrelevant to sociocultural interpretation because they cannot be empirically verified; for example, metaphysical or theological interpretations of the meaning of the universe. See also his discussion of "empathetic," "subjective," or "emotional" interpretation (Weber, 1975, pp. 179-184). There are other varieties of interpretation which are irrelevant to sociocultural interpretation because they are utterly unproblematical; see, for example, Weber's remarks on *"aktuelles Verstehen"* or "quotidian understanding" (Weber, 1975, pp. 153-154). There are other varieties of interprion which may prove to be useful preliminaries to the development of a sociocultural interpretation, even though they do not constitute such an interpretation; for example, "axiological" interpretation and "dialectical" interpretation (see Weber, 1968, pp. 151, 155-156, 245-253).

16. Weber's analysis of the concept of a rule includes a discussion of the relationship between the concept of "following a rule" and the concepts of meaning, interpretation, and understanding. It contains an explanation of the sense in which the notion of following a rule—a rule of a game, for example—is a constitutive sociological concept. This discussion provides the foundation for the position that Weber will sketch later in *Economy and Society*. It also anticipates the later theories of language games developed by Wittgenstein and his followers, the logical analyses of the concept of a rule and closely related concepts in Anglo-American analytical philosophy—for example, the work of J. L. Austin, H. L. A. Hart, Max Black, and John Rawls—and the notion of *Lebenswelt* or life-world employed in the phenomenological sociologies of Alfred Schutz and his many followers, imitators, and epigones.

17. In the conclusion of his important essay on the genesis of Weber's methodology, Tenbruck makes a claim which now can be regarded only as a curiosity. "As a whole, Max Weber's methodology has nothing of substantive importance to tell us" (Tenbruck, 1959, pp. 625-626). This view of the contemporary irrelevance of Weber's methodology seems to be radically mistaken. The Verstehen thesis as analyzed above, sketched in the critique of Stammler, and explicitly formulated by Weber in the 1913 *Logos* essay and the first chapter of *Economy and Society*, is a fundamental metatheoretical postulate of a number of contemporary sociocultural methodologies: phenomenological social science (see, for example,

Schutz, 1962, 1964, 1967; Schutz and Luckmann, 1973), ethno-methodology (see, for example, Garfinkel, 1967; Filmer et al., 1973), the sociology of everyday life (see, for example, Douglas, 1970), and what might be called "Wittgensteinian" or "Oxford" social science (see, for example, Winch, 1963; Louch, 1966; MacIntyre, 1962, 1971; and Wittgenstein, 1967).

18. Although his sketch of the Verstehen thesis as the solution to the constitutive problem is the principal focus of the critique of Stammler, it is not its exclusive focus. Throughout the critique, Weber repeatedly returns to the defense of a proposition that is a logical consequence of the Verstehen thesis. This proposition articulates one of the basic metatheoretical postulates of the inquiry that Weber will later call "interpretive sociology." In any explanation of the problematical properties of a sociocultural phenomenon, it is necessary to take into account the ideas that are in the minds of the actors. This is Weber's way of expressing the point. Perhaps it can be formulated more precisely if we introduce a distinction between a sociocultural explanans and a sociocultural explanandum. A sociocultural explanandum may be understood as a proposition that identifies the problematical features of some sociocultural phenomenon. A sociocultural explanans may be understood as a proposition that accounts for or explains the problematical features of some sociocultural phenomenon, features that are identified by a sociocultural explanandum. Given this distinction, Weber's point may be stated in the following way. Any sociocultural explanans must employ an S-predicate which is truly ascribed if and only if the Verstehen criterion is satisfied. In other words, every sociocultural explanans must employ some Verstehen predicate. Why? Consider Weber's commitment to the Verstehen thesis as the solution to the constitutive problem. Given the Verstehen thesis, the explanandum must employ some V-predicate. Since the explanans is intended to account for the problematical features of the sociocultural phenomenon as identified by the explanandum, it follows that the explanans must also employ this V-predicate. Or, as Weber expresses the matter, in an explanation of a sociocultural phenomenon, "processes of consciousness" are included in the causal chain, the chain that links the sociocultural phenomenon to the conditions for its existence. Weber returns to this thesis in *Economy and Society*. For an excellent discussion of

the importance of this thesis in the critique of Stammler and its bearing on Weber's view of interpretive sociology—in particular, an interpretive sociology of law—see Loos (1970).

References

Abel, Theodore
1948   "The Operation called *Verstehen*," *American Journal of Sociology*, volume 54

Brinkmann, Carl
1950   *Wirtschaftsformen ünd Lebensformen*, Tübingen

Bruun, H. H.
1972   *Science, Values and Politics in Max Weber's Methodology*, Copenhagen

Burger, Thomas
1976   *Max Weber's Theory of Concept Formation*, Durham, N.C.

Douglas, Jack D. (ed.)
1970   *Understanding Everyday Life*, Chicago

Filmer, Paul, et al.
1973   *New Directions in Sociological Theory*, Cambridge, Mass.

Friedrich, Carl J.
1963   *The Philosophy of Law in Historical Perspective*, second edition, Chicago

Garfinkel, Harold
1967   *Studies in Ethnomethodology*, Englewood Cliffs, N.J.

Gouldner, Alvin W.
1973   *For Sociology*, New York

Henrich, Dieter
1952   *Die Einheit der Wissenschaftslehre Max Webers*, Tübingen

Hughes, H. Stuart
1958   *Consciousness and Society: The Reorientation of European Social Thought 1890-1930*, New York

Jaspers, Karl
1926   *Max Weber, Rede bei der Heidelberger Studentschaft am 17 Juli 1920 veranstalteten Trauerfeier*, Munich
1958a   *Max Weber, Politiker, Forscher, Philosoph*, Munich
1958b   "Philosophische Autobiographie," in *Philosophie und die Welt*, Munich

Kantorowicz, Hermann
1909   *Zur Lehre vom richtigen Recht*, Berlin and Leipzig

Kuhn, Thomas S.
1970   *The Structure of Scientific Revolutions*, second edition, enlarged, Chicago

Larenz, Karl
1931   *Rechts-und Staatsphilosophie der Gegenwart*, Berlin
1960   *Methodenlehre der Rechtswissenschaft*, Berlin

Leat, Diana
1972   "Misunderstanding Verstehen," *Sociological Review*, volume 20

Lindenlaub, Dieter
1967   *Richtungskämpfe im Verein für Sozialpolitik*, volume 2. *Vierteljahrsschrift für Sozial und Wirtschaftsgeschichte*, Beiheft 53, Wiesbaden

Loos, Fritz
1970   *Zur Wert-und Rechtslehre Max Webers*, Tübingen

Louch, A. R.
1966   *Explanation and Human Action*, Berkeley and Los Angeles

MacIntyre, A. D.
1962   "A Mistake about Causality in Social Science," in P. Laslett and W. G. Runciman (eds.), *Philosophy Politics, and Society*, 2nd series, Oxford
1971   *Against the Self-Images of the Age*, New York

Malinowski, Bronislaw
1967   *A Diary in the Strict Sense of the Term*, New York

Martindalte, Don
1959   "Sociological Theory and the Idealtype," in Llewellyn Gross (ed.), *Symposium on Sociological Theory*, New York

Menger, Carl
   1883   *Untersuchungen über die Methode der Sozialwissen-schaften und der politischen Oekonomie insbesondere*, Vienna
   1884   *Die Irrtümer des Historismus in der Nationaloekonomie*, Vienna

Mitzman, Arthur
   1973   *Sociology and Estrangement. Three Sociologists of Imperial Germany*, New York

Oakes, Guy
   1977   "The Verstehen Thesis and the Foundations of Max Weber's Methodology," *History and Theory*, volume 16

Popper, Karl R.
   1963   *The Open Society and its Enemies*, volume 2, New York

Rickert, Heinrich
   1902   *Die Grenzen der naturwissenschaftlichen Begriffs-bildung*, Tübingen (5th edition, 1929)
   1926   "Max Weber und seine Stellung zur Wissenschaft," *Logos*, volume 15

Ringer, Fritz
   1969   *The Decline of the German Mandarins: The German Academic Community, 1890-1933*, Cambridge, Mass.

Ritzel, G.
   1950   *Schmoller versus Menger*, Frankfurt

Runciman, W. G.
   1972   *A Critique of Max Weber's Philosophy of Social Science*, Cambridge, Eng.

Schelting, Alexander von
   1934   *Max Webers Wissenschaftslehre*, Tübingen

Schmoller, Gustav
   1883   "Zur Methodologie der Staats-und Sozialwissenschaf-ten," *Schmoller's Jahrbuch*, N.F., volume 7

Schutz, Alfred
   1962   *Collected Papers*, volume 1, The Hague
   1964   *Collected Papers*, volume 2, The Hague
   1967   *The Phenomenology of the Social World*, Evanston, Ill.

Schutz, Alfred, and Thomas Luckmann
1973   *The Structures of the Life-World*, Evanston, Ill.

Stammler, Rudolf
1902   *Die Lehre vom richtigen Recht*, Berlin
1906   *Wirtschaft und Recht nach der materialistischen Ges-chichtsauffassung. Eine Sozialphilosophische Unter-suchung*, 2nd, revised edition, Leipzig (4th edition, 1921)
1911   *Theorie der Rechtswissenschaft*, Halle
1922   *Lehrbuch der Rechtsphilosophie*, Berlin

Tenbruck, Friedrich
1959   "Die Genesis der Methodologie Max Webers," *Kölner Zeitschrift für Soziologie und Sozialpsychologie*, volume 2

Troeltsch, Ernst
1922   *Der Historismus und seine Probleme*, Tübingen
1925   *Deutscher Geist und Westeuropa*, Tübingen

Weber, Marianne
1900   *Fichte's Sozialismus und sein Verhältnis zu Marx'schen Doktrin*, Tübingen
1926   *Max Weber: Ein Lebensbild*, Tübingen
1975   *Max Weber: A Biography* (tr. and ed. by Henry Zohn), New York (translation of Marianne Weber, 1926)

Weber, Max
1903   "Roscher's 'historische Methode,'" *Schmoller's Jahr-buch*, volume 25
1904   "Die 'Objektivität' sozialwissenschaftlicher und sozial-politischer Erkenntnis," *Archiv für Sozialwissenschaft und Sozialpolitik*, volume 19
1905   "Knies und das Irrationalitätsproblem," *Schmoller's Jahrbuch*, volume 29
1906a   "Knies und das Irrationalitätsproblem (forts.)," *Schmol-ler's Jahrbuch*, volume 30
1906b   "Kritische Studien auf dem Gebiet der kulturwissen-schaftlichen Logik," *Archiv für Sozialwissenschaft und Sozialpolitik*, volume 22
1907   "R. Stammler's 'Überwindung' der materialistischen Geschichtsauffassung," *Archiv für Sozialwissenschaft*

und Sozialpolitik, volume 24

1913   "Über einige Kategorien der verstehenden Soziologie," *Logos*, volume 4

1949   *Methodology of the Social Sciences* (tr. by Edward Shils and Henry Finch), Glencoe, Ill. (translation of Weber 1904 and 1906b)

1964   "Gutachten zur Werturteilsdiskussion im Ausschuss des Vereins für Sozialpolitik," in Eduard Baumgarten, *Max Weber: Werk und Person*, Tübingen

1968   *Gesammelte Aufsätze zur Wissenschaftslehre*, 3rd edition, Tübingen

1974   *Max Weber on Universities* (translated, edited, and with an introductory note by Edward Shils), Chicago

1975   *Roscher and Knies: The Logical Problems of Historical Economics* (translated with an introductory essay by Guy Oakes), New York

Winch, Peter

1963   *The Idea of a Social Science*, London

Wittgenstein, Ludwig

1967   "Bermerkungen über Frazer's *The Golden Bough*," *Synthese*, volume 17

Wrong, Dennis (ed.)

1970   *Max Weber*, Englewood Cliffs, N.J.

Critique of Stammler

Max Weber

Stammler's "Refutation" of the Materialist Conception of History

Preliminary Remarks

Consider the "second, revised edition" of a book which has exercised a great influence upon the discussion of the fundamental questions of social science.[1] It is undeniable that the principal effect of Stammler's book has been the production of confusion. But it is also indubitable that the book has exerted an extremely stimulating influence. To argue that the existence of such a book has no scientific basis is a disagreeable undertaking. But that is what shall be done here, and moreover with uncompromising candor. At this point, therefore, two things are needed: first, some reservations; and then a brief justification for this project, which at the outset will only be very general. First, the following point should be made clearly and unconditionally. To a great extent, Stammler's work exhibits scholarship, acuteness, an idealistic aspiration for knowledge, and even "imagination." However this is precisely the grotesque feature of the book: the disparity between the valuable conclusions that are established and the

59

atrocious ostentation of the technique used to establish them. It is *almost* as if a manufacturer set in motion all the achievements of technology in an immense factory of the most modern construction, employing a prodigious outlay of capital and innumerable laborers, all in order to produce atmospheric *air* (gaseous, not liquid!).

It is "almost" as if this were the case. And here a second reservation is needed. As I just noted, there is no doubt that the book contains *specific* points of enduring value, points in which one may legitimately take pride. We should identify these points conscientiously and, wherever possible, emphasize them. However—regardless of how favorably these points may be evaluated—they are, unfortunately, only of very limited significance in comparison with the extravagant pretensions of the book. Some of these points would have their proper place in a monograph on the relationship between conceptual schemes in jurisprudence and economics. Others would find their proper place in a monograph on the formal presuppositions of social ideals. Both works would certainly retain an enduring interest and value. But it is obvious that they would not produce the great sensation generated by this book, which employs these elements for such pretentious purposes. The valuable elements of the book disappear in a thicket of apparent truths, half truths, and truths incorrectly formulated. They are concealed within unclear formulations of covert falsities. They are hidden by sophistry and scholastic fallacies. For these reasons, criticism of the book is an infinitely tedious and extremely lengthy undertaking. In view of the essentially negative results of this critique, it is also a distasteful task. Nevertheless, the analysis of a relatively large number of specific theses is quite unavoidable. This is necessary in order to establish the utter invalidity of the arguments Stammler uses to support them, arguments which he presents with the most staggering confidence.

Of course it is also possible for a critic to exaggerate the defects of a book. In the work of any writer, it is possible to identify points at which a given problem is not thought through to a conclusion or points at which a thesis is carelessly stated, unclear, or obviously false. This is particularly the case when those of us who are not professional logicians find it necessary to deal with logical problems in the substantive interests of our professional disciplines. Consider the sorts of logical issues that are inessential or relatively inessential for our concrete substantive problems. Especially in cases of this sort, it is unavoidable that the use of the conceptual apparatus of the professional logician will easily lead to errors. This is because we do not employ this conceptual apparatus regularly in our everyday research. Facility in the employment of these concepts is impossible unless they are used regularly. But consider also the following. First, it is Stammler who *represents himself* as an "epistemologist." And in addition—as we shall see—the present essay is concerned with arguments to which Stammler himself gives the principal emphasis. Finally—and this should not be forgotten—we are discussing a *second edition*. Therefore the conditions which this book should satisfy are altogether different from the requirements we would impose upon a "first draft." This is the point that obviously calls for the most severe and unqualified criticism: the fact that Stammler has published such a text in the guise of a revised edition. The severity of the ensuing criticism is not a response to the book itself, but rather a response to a second edition of this quality. In discussing a "first draft"—and this is what Stammler's first edition presented—we would be content to follow the wisdom according to which it is always easier to criticize a book than to write one. But what of a second, "revised" edition which appears almost ten years after the publication of the first edition? In this case, we should expect criticism from the author himself. Especially in discussions of *logical* problems, it is inexcusable to utterly ignore—as Stammler does— the relevant professional literature in logic.

One final point: Stammler represents himself as an advocate of "critical idealism." In both ethics and epistemology, he wants to be acknowledged as the most authentic of the neo-Kantians. Given the limits of the ensuing criticism, it will be impossible to provide a detailed analysis of the vulgar errors in the interpretation of Kantian doctrine on which Stammler bases this pretension. In any case, the advocates of "critical idealism" have every reason to disclaim the authenticity of Stammler's neo-Kantian pretensions. This is because the definitive theses of Stammler's work approximate all too closely arguments which support the following archaic doctrine of naturalism. In the criticism of naturalistic dogmatism, the epistemologist is obliged to choose between two modes of demonstration: "either a crude and sophistical fallacy or a subtle sleight of hand."

Stammler's Account of Historical Materialism

As he repeatedly emphasizes, the purpose of Stammler's work[2] is to provide a scientific "refutation" of the "materialist conception of history." Before proceeding any further, therefore, two questions should be posed. First, how does Stammler conceive this conception of history? And second, on *exactly what grounds* does Stammler base his scientific criticism of this conception of history? In order to answer these questions as clearly as possible, it will be useful to make a short digression.

In our time, there is a pronounced emphasis upon the significance of religious phenomena in cultural history. In view of this increasing tendency, let us imagine an author who advocates the following position. "History is nothing more than a product of the *religious* attitudes and struggles of mankind. In the final analysis, all the phenomena of cultural life—and especially the phenomena of political and economic life—are simply consequences of religious interests and attitudes. All events, even political and economic events, are ultimately reflections of the specific attitudes which men adopt on religious issues. In the last analysis, therefore, all cultural phenomena are merely forms in which religious forces and ideas are expressed. The following, therefore, is a condition for the possibility of a scientific explanation of an historical event or process: it is necessary to identify the religious ideas which are causally responsible for it. Moreover, this sort of explanation is the only possible way in which the *totality* of 'social' evolution can be scientifically comprehended as an *entity* which functions according to established laws (see Stammler, the bottom of p. 66 and the top of p. 67): that is, in the same fashion that the natural sciences comprehend 'natural' evolution."

Consider now an "empiricist" who raises the following objection. It is obvious that there are numerous concrete phenomena of political and economic life for which no religious motivation of any sort can be identified. We can imagine that our "spiritualist" might offer this reply. "There is no doubt that every single event has more than just one single cause. In consequence, there is no question at all that within the causal chain numerous *individual* events and motivations can be identified as causes, even though they have no religious character of any sort. However everyone knows that it is possible to continue the causal regress ad infinitum. If this is undertaken (Stammler, p. 67, line 11), a religious motive will *always* be discovered at some point. It is this motive which has the 'decisive' influence upon the manner in which men live. In the final analysis, *it follows that* all other variables in human life can be traced back to variations in religious attitudes (Stammler, p. 31, line 26). Since they are only reflections of variations in religious attitudes, these variables have no independent, real existence at all (Stammler, p. 30, eleventh line from the bottom). This is because every change in the independent religious variable produces a corresponding, parallel change in every domain of the conduct of life (Stammler, p. 24, line 5). Therefore religious factors are invariably the exclusive causal forces in social life and also—consciously or unconsciously—in the career of individual human beings. Given a *complete* knowledge of the 'uniform relations' of the causal chain, these decisive religious factors will invariably appear (Stammler, p. 67, line 20). How could it be otherwise? The external forms of political and economic life do not exist as autonomous, isolated worlds. They do not have their own definitive causes (Stammler, p. 26, sixth line from the bottom). Nor do they even exist as independent entities (Stammler, p. 29, sixth line from the bottom). On the contrary, only in the interest of an abstraction from the totality of life as a whole is it possible to conceive them as independent 'isolated entities' " (Stammler, p. 68, line 11).

The "sound common sense" of our "empiricist" would probably lead him to raise the following objection at this point. As regards both the variety and the dimensions of the reciprocal causal influence of various sorts of "social phenomena" upon one another, it is impossible to make any general, a priori claims. Both the existence and also the variety and the extent of reciprocal causation can be established only by examining specific cases. Then it might be possible—perhaps through the comparison of cases that are really or apparently similar—to do more than merely establish the extent to which a given social phenomenon is a consequence of religious causes. It might be possible to establish "generalizations." But note: they are certainly not generalizations about the causal significance of "the religious" *as such* for "social life" *as such*. That is a vague and mistaken problematic. These generalizations would articulate the causal relationship between *classes* of religious cultural elements and other *classes* of cultural elements. It would be necessary to identify both classes of cultural elements quite precisely. And our "empiricist" would probably add the following point to this objection. The various independent "problematics" that are employed in order to classify cultural phenomena—as "political," "religious," "economic," and so on—are obviously one-sided. They serve only one purpose: the "economy" of scientific research. They are employed whenever they are of some practical value for this purpose.

But consider cultural evolution as a whole or a "totality," in the scientific sense of this expression. That is, consider it from the standpoint of "what we value as worth knowing." Scientific knowledge of this "totality" is possible only through synthesis, only by progressing from a "monocausal" to a "comprehensive conception." Such knowledge can never be established through the futile attempt to represent historical structures as if they were exclusively determined by artificially isolated elements that are merely products of fabrication. Given this standpoint, the causal "regress" obviously leads nowhere. Regress as far as you like, even to the dawn of "prehistory." To terminate the causal regress by placing "religious" elements in relief from the totality of phenomena and ascribing a preeminent status to them is invariably to accept a "monocausal" position. Precisely the same would be the case if a preeminent status had been ascribed to the "religious" elements of the historical stage from which the regress was begun. In specific cases, it may be of the greatest heuristic value to limit the investigation to the discovery of the causal importance of "religious" factors. This depends exclusively upon whether the investigation is "successful" in the discovery of new theoretical knowledge. But consider the thesis according to which the *totality* of cultural phenomena is, "in the final analysis," *exclusively* determined by religious motives. This is an insupportable hypothesis. Moreover, it is inconsistent with established "facts."

Our "historical spiritualist," however, would not accept the "sound common sense" on which these arguments are based. Let us consider how he would reply to them. "Consider the doubt that the causally decisive religious factor can invariably be *identified*. Suppose that this doubt is taken seriously. Then, in principle, it casts doubt upon the legitimacy of any method which undertakes to establish nomological knowledge from *one* point of view (Stammler, p. 66, line 11). Every scientific inquiry, however, is subject to the law of causality. This law has the status of an axiom. *Therefore* every scientific inquiry must be committed to the following basic presupposition: there is *one* general law according to which all individual phenomena are exhaustively correlated. Independent of this presupposition, any claim to nomological knowledge is senseless (Stammler, see the fifth line from the bottom of p. 67 and the top of p. 68). Consider the postulate according to which all social phenomena can be traced back to religious motives. This postulate does not claim that the attempt to identify these motives always succeeds, or at least succeeds most of the time. It does not even claim that the attempt is ever entirely successful (Stammler, p. 69, eighth line from the bottom). The postulate is not a mere statement of fact. It is a *method* (Stammler, p. 68, sixth line from the bottom). Therefore the objection that the postulate is an illegitimate generalization—because it is derived from individual sociohistorical events—is based on a *conceptual* error. The postulate was not established by generalizations of this sort. It was established a priori by posing the following question. '*In general*, under what conditions are legitimate generalizations possible?' (Stammler, p. 69, line 3).

As a method of establishing theoretical knowledge, generalization is based on the assumption that there is one, ultimate, *unified* point of view, a problematic which must undertake to represent the ultimate, fundamental unity of social life. Otherwise theoretical knowledge is impossible. The foregoing postulate, therefore, is a systematic and *universally valid method* for answering the following question: *What are the general conditions for the possibility of a scientific conception* of the concrete events of social life? (Stammler, p. 69, line 12, *seq.*). This postulate is a basic *formal principle* of social research (p. 69, line 24). Historical *facts*, however, cannot be employed to attack or 'refute' a *method*. As regards the question of its validity *in principle*, it obviously does not make the slightest difference whether such a *formal* principle can be *employed* successfully in a given case. Often it even happens that the use of the most indubitable and generally valid axioms for establishing nomological knowledge fails to produce results that are satisfying (Stammler, p. 69, tenth line from the bottom). This fundamental principle is completely independent of *any given substantive property* of social processes. It would remain valid even if *no single* fact could actually be explained by applying the principle consistently.

This point concerns the peculiar difficulty which arises when the principle of causality is employed to investigate human social life instead of 'nature.' There is no reason to devote an independent discussion to this difficulty (Stammler, top of p. 70). If, however, the *formal* principle of *all* theoretical knowledge is to have any application at all within the domain of social life, then the foregoing postulate *must* have a logical status which corresponds to its formal character. And that is possible *only* by reducing *all* nomological regularities within the domain of the social to one 'fundamental regularity': causal dependence upon the religious factor. Consider, therefore, the proposition that 'in the final analysis' social life is a product of *religious* motives. A scientific conception of the social world as an *entity* that functions 'according to mechanical laws' is possible only by 'deriving' *all* social phenomena from *religious* causes. It follows that it is *altogether* impossible to refute this proposition 'empirically.' Nor is this proposition a mere generalization of factual data (Stammler, the bottom of p. 68 and the top of p. 69). On the contrary, this proposition is a consequence of the nature of our thought insofar as its purpose is the discovery of *nomological* knowledge. And this must be the purpose of any science that employs the law of causality. To attack this proposition, therefore, is to attack *the theoretical goal of this sort of knowledge*. In consequence, anyone who undertakes this attack must ground it in the *theory of knowledge*. He must ask: what is 'nomological' knowledge of social life? What is the *import* of this sort of knowledge (Stammler, p. 69, line 22)? Consider the conditions under which it is possible to attack the *method* of deriving all social phenomena from a single, *uniform* factor. This sort of attack is possible only if the *concept* of 'nomological regularity' *itself* becomes problematical. Only under this condition is it possible to raise the question of the justification of the following proposition: 'in the last analysis' the causally decisive factors are religious motives."

"Until now, however"—our historical spiritualist is obviously not yet familiar with the work of *Stammler*—"no one has made this attempt. On the contrary, what we find is a war of petty skirmishes over concrete matters of fact. But this is not germane to the principle itself" (Stammler, p. 63, second line from the bottom).

How shall the sound common sense of our "empiricist" respond to these claims? Unless he can be reduced to a befuddled silence through confusion and bewilderment, I think he will treat this position—be it naive or audacious—as a species of *scholastic mystification*. With the same "logic," he would argue, the following "methodological principle" could also be established. "In the final analysis," "social life" is a consequence of the size of the skull, or the effects of sun spots, or indigestion. This principle remains incontestable as long as it has not been refuted by an epistemological investigation which would establish the "meaning" of the concept of "social nomological regularity." Personally, I would say that "sound common sense" is correct on this point.

Obviously *Stammler* thinks *otherwise*. In the foregoing account of "historical spiritualism"—its verbosity was intentional, quite in the style of Stammler—it is only necessary to substitute the word "material" (in the sense of "economic") in all the passages in which the word "religious" appears. As anyone can establish by examining the passages in Stammler's book that I have placed in parentheses, the result—it is, for the most part, a literal rendition, but it is always faithful to Stammler's text—is Stammler's view of the "materialist conception of history." At this juncture, we are concerned only with the following point. With a single reservation, Stammler accepts this view of the "materialist conception of history" as *absolutely valid.*[3] And the reservation? Stammler—his feet planted firmly on the ground of "epistemology"—is the man who will "conquer" this heretofore undefeated Goliath. The "refutation," however, will not establish that this conception of history is substantively "incorrect." It is only *"incomplete."* And it is not "incomplete" in the sense of being "one-sided." It is only "unfinished." This "completion" and "conquest," therefore, will proceed as follows. By employing a series of conceptual manipulations, Stammler proves that the "nomological regularity of the social"—in the sense of a "fundamental unity" of both social life *and* knowledge of social life (as we shall see, Stammler conflates the two)—is conceptually possible as a "formal principle" only in the "universe of purposes": only as a constitutive principle which defines the "form of human societal existence," only as a "unified formal idea which serves as the guiding light for all empirical, social *endeavors.*"

At this point, we are not concerned with the question of whether Stammler's representation of the "materialist conception of history" is *sound.* From *The Communist Manifesto* to the work of the contemporary epigones of Marx, this theory has passed through very different forms. Therefore let us admit a priori that the following assumption is both possible and probable. One of Stammler's versions of the theory at least approximates the "materialist conception of history."[4] And even if this is not the case, a critic of the theory would still be justified in attempting to construct the form which a self-consistent version of the theory "should have had." Here we are not concerned with the theory itself, but rather with Stammler. At this point, therefore, we shall only pose a question concerning the "theory of knowledge" to which, *Stammler* claims, the materialist conception of history is committed. We are not concerned with the problem of whether Stammler is justified in making this claim. On the contrary, we are concerned with the following issue: How does Stammler develop and ground this theory? It is a theory of knowledge which Stammler regards as incorrigible, or rather as corrigible only on the basis of his own theory of knowledge. Have we been unfair to Stammler? Perhaps he is not so fully committed to historical materialism as we have prima facie assumed. In order to answer these questions, let us examine the introductory, "epistemological" sections of his book.

Stammler's "Theory of Knowledge"

In order to gain some insight into Stammler's idiosyncratic mode of argumentation, a detailed analysis of at least some of the arguments contained in the introductory part of his book is necessary by way of illustration. Therefore let us take this initial section of the book and analyze it into a series of propositions. Then we shall consider how these propositions are related.   On the first few pages of the text (pp. 3-6), we find the following claims. Every "single piece of careful research" remains valueless and "fortuitous": (1) unless it can be identified as a "dependent *variable of* a general nomological regularity"; (2) unless it *satisfies* a "universally valid criterion of knowledge"; (3) unless it is "founded upon" a "basic nomological regularity"; (4) unless it is based upon a "uniform and *unconditional problematic*" (Stammler, p. 3); (5) unless it is based on insight "into a *universally valid*, nomological correlation" (Stammler, p. 4). This is because (6) the assumption that such a nomological regularity exists is a "presupposition" of any inquiry which "*transcends* the brute facts established by observation." (7) The real question, therefore, is the following: "Can a general *nomological regularity* be established in human social *life* in the same way that the nomological regularity of nature has been established as the foundation of the natural sciences?" (Stammler, p. 5). Up to this point, unfortunately, no one has been capable of answering this question. (8) This question "concerns the *nomological regularity* of all *knowledge* of social phenomena." (9) *"In practice,"* however, the question concerning the *"identification* of the ultimate nomological regularity on which *knowledge* of social life is dependent" (!) "emanates directly into the *fundamental conception* of the relation between the individual and the totality" (!). And in fact "the aspiration ... for the *nomological transformation* of social *life* exists ... It is called: the social question." (10) Consider *"scientific* knowledge of the *nomological regularity* which is *valid* for human social life in general. It *follows that* this sort of knowledge is a condition for the possibility of *structuring* human collective life in a *lawlike* fashion."

Enough for the present. Stammler claims that anyone who uses the expression *"nomological* processes" must, above all, know "what he *really* wants to *say"* (Stammler, p. 4). In view of the foregoing patchwork of claims, each of which employs the concept of "nomological regularity," it is regrettable that Stammler has ignored his own advice so completely. On the one hand, it is obvious that almost each of the above ten propositions concerns a different issue. On the other hand, it is just as indubitable that the reading of Stammler's book establishes the following astonishing fact: Stammler has deceived himself. It is one and the same problem that is invariably under discussion. The only variation is in the language employed. How is this possible in a work of such pretensions? It is a consequence of the unparalleled vagueness and ambiguity of Stammler's language.

Let us have another look at the foregoing ten propositions. I have taken them from Stammler's text because they articulate his principal theses. The sense of proposition (1) is quite obscure. It is not clear what the expression "dependent *variable of* a nomological regularity" could mean. Does this mean that significant pieces of research can be undertaken only in order to derive general (universal) nomological regularities from them (nomothetic knowledge)? Or does it mean that the causal interpretation of concrete constellations is impossible without the use of general (nomological) knowledge (historical knowledge)? Stammler may have either or both of these points in mind—at least this is what proposition (7) suggests. According to this proposition, the "principal question" is allegedly the following. Can laws of "social life"—that is how I am inclined to interpret this extremely vague text—be established in the same way that "natural laws" are established for "inanimate" nature? Consider propositions (3) and (6). They claim that a foundation upon a "basic nomological regularity" is a *necessary* presupposition" of all valid knowledge of single "facts." These propositions suggest that the rationale behind those theses which refer to the universal validity of the category of causality (in the sense of "nomological regularity") must be altogether unsatisfactory.

On the other hand, Stammler surprises us in propositions (2) and (8). They are not concerned with the "nomological regularity" of the *event* which is the object of knowledge, but rather with the "nomological regularity" of *knowledge*. These propositions are not concerned with "laws" which empirically govern the *object* of knowledge or the world of "objects," "laws" the discovery of which is the task of induction (see proposition [6] and Stammler, the bottom of p. 4: "proceeding from single observations" so that "specific facts can achieve the status of necessary truths"). On the contrary, they are concerned with *norms* which are valid within the domain of *knowledge*. This is the only sense that can be made of the expressions "universally *valid* criterion of *knowledge*" (proposition [2]) and the "nomological regularity of all our *knowledge* of the social" (proposition [8]). At this point, Stammler conflates "norms of logic" and "laws of nature." And, as if this were not enough, the (according to proposition [5]) indispensable *insight* into the *correlation* between facts (a concrete object) is completely confused with insight into *"nomological regularity"* (an abstraction). If "nomological regularity" is to be understood as the nomological regularity of nature, then the two kinds of insight are antithetical. If, on the other hand, "nomological regularity" is to be understood as a "norm" of knowledge, then the two expressions refer to two distinctly different logical relations. Moreover, the predicate "universally *valid"* is also ascribed to this "nomological correlation" (proposition [5]).

Stammler is not concerned here with the "validity" of empirical-scientific *propositions* about a purely "factual" correlation. At least this is suggested by proposition (3). As it stands, proposition (3) is quite unintelligible. It concerns the necessity of a "foundation" constituted by a *"uniform problematic,"* a problematic that is *"unconditional."* Of course it is true that both the *classification* of facts into concrete correlations and the derivation of "nomological regularities" from facts are usually undertaken from the standpoint of distinctive "problematics." The division of labor in most of the individual sciences is based on this practice. But it does not follow that there is *one* "unconditional" problematic for all empirical disciplines. Suppose that Stammler had in mind here the principle of quantification and mathematical form. This is certainly not an exceptionless feature of all the so-called "natural sciences," in the academic or departmental sense of this expression. Moreover the differential and *multiple* "problematics" in terms of which they conceive reality is a distinguishing feature of the disciplines usually called the "sociocultural sciences." Finally, there is absolutely no justification for identifying *"uniform problematic"* in this sense with a fundamental *"nomological regularity"* which can be ascribed to all sciences. Let us even suppose that one wanted to call the category of causality, which is constitutive to all sciences, a "problematic"—more on this later. In this case, consider the historical disciplines. They explain *concrete* objects in the causal regress by reference to other concrete objects. Perhaps one could speak here of the "nomological regularity" of the event in a very special sense: as one of the general "presuppositions" of the historical disciplines. But "nomological regularity" certainly cannot be identified as the *ground* of the *coherence* of "specific observations" in these disciplines.

Although Stammler conflates "uniformity," "nomological regularity," "correlation," and "problematic" with extravagant naïveté, it is obvious that these expressions have fundamentally different referents. The dimensions of the confusion that Stammler produces finally become clear when we examine proposition (9) and learn which "problematic" he really has in mind. The "ultimate *nomological regularity*" of social life "emanates in" the "fundamental *conception* of the relation between the individual and the totality." Stammler's language, again, is extremely vague. Suppose we examine this proposition as it stands, stated in an altogether slovenly fashion. The following question obviously arises. Is this "conception" concerned with the scientific *explanation* of the "empirical" relationship between "concrete matters of fact" and the "totality"? Or is Stammler taking a fatal plunge into the "world of values," the world of *axiology*? Consider proposition (10), according to which "insight into the nomological regularity that is valid for human social life" is a condition for "the possibility of structuring human social life in a nomological fashion." As it stands, this proposition could be understood in such a way that the "insight" concerns the laws which govern the *event*.

Suppose that it is possible to discover "laws" of social events that are similar to the "laws of nature." Economists have repeatedly attempted to do just this. *In that case*, these laws would have the same status in relation to the "purposeful" regulation of social events and the ability to influence them in accordance with our intentions that knowledge of the laws of "inanimate" nature occupies in relation to the technological mastery of the natural world. Moreover there is no doubt that knowledge of these laws would be just as valuable as knowledge of the laws of nature. But even the reference to the "social question" in proposition (9) shows that—at least in the context of this proposition—the "nomological transformation" of social life cannot be understood simply as a sociopolitical process of this sort. It is not a process which is exclusively concerned with "laws" of *events*—like laws of nature—the validity of which is established empirically. On the contrary, it obviously must be understood as a transformation which satisfies the requirements of *axiological* laws: *practical norms.*

It is true enough that Stammler sometimes uses the same word in the same sentence with two different meanings. And he does this with complete composure. In view of the foregoing, nevertheless, we are obliged to reach the following conclusion. In this context, the "validity" of "nomological regularity" is to be understood in an *imperative* sense. Therefore "insight" into this "nomological regularity" is knowledge of a "precept." Moreover it is the "ultimate" and "fundamental" precept of all social life. In other words, Stammler has actually taken the fatal plunge into the "world of values." Thus we find ourselves on the brink of the following confusions: law of nature, category of logic, and imperative of action; "universality," "uniformity," "correlation," and "problematic"; validity as empirical necessity, as a methodological principle, as a logical norm, and as a practical norm. All this and more is presented in a thoroughly confused fashion at the beginning of a book in which Stammler's adversary will be defeated on "epistemological" grounds. Surely no satisfactory results can be expected from such a beginning.

But perhaps Stammler is only *pretending to be* so confused on all these points. As a matter of fact, his book is certainly not free from the attempt to produce "sensations," in particular the sensation of "suspense." Perhaps his intention is to allow unclarity of expression to predominate in these introductory pages. Then, gradually, logical clarity and conceptual order will follow. The reader, languishing in this chaos of darkness, will be led step by step until he is prepared to receive the final, enlightening word that will resolve all these difficulties successfully. If one reads further into the "Introduction" (pp. 3–20), however, he does not find that the level of confusion abates. It increases.

At the bottom of page 12 and the top of p. 13, we again find ambiguous expressions like "social teaching" and "uniform fundamental conception" of social life used in order to represent the "insight" into "nomological regularity" (Stammler, p. 13, penultimate paragraph) as a "standard" according to which all the *single observations* (note!) of social *history* (note!) "can be consistently conceived, evaluated, and ordered." In the last quoted remark (the penultimate paragraph of p. 13), we find an obvious value judgment concerning the purpose of "social science." But in the first two quoted remarks (from the bottom of p. 12 and the top of p. 13),[5] the reader has the impression that Stammler is concerned with theoretical knowledge. Examine, however, the following claim on page 14. This is meant to clarify the foundation of "social *philosophy*" (Concerning which, see Stammler, the bottom of p. 13). "Consider the person who discusses the nomological regularity of social life" (ambiguous—see the above remarks), "social evolution" (theoretical), "social injustice" (normative), "and the possibility or impossibility"[6] (theoretical) "of its cure" (normative), "who introduces (!) laws of socioeconomic phenomena" (formally, a theoretical concept), discusses "social conflicts" (formally, also a theoretical concept), and "affirms or denies" (theoretical: see note 6), "progress in the domain of human societal existence" (normative). "In order to avoid matters that are irrelevant (?) and subjective" (this applies only to *value* judgments), he "must, above all, clarify the definitive features of socio*scientific* knowledge" (in other words, not socio*philosophical* knowledge, which Stammler was discussing up to this point). Consider this claim. In each of its parts, the discussion swings, in pendulum-like fashion, back and forth between the question of the knowledge of facts and the question of their evaluation.

Later Stammler claims (at the bottom of p. 15): "The universally *valid* (note!) *nomological regularity* of social life which unfolds in history" (in other words, the "nomological regularity" of the object of knowledge) "entails (!) the uniform (?) and (?) universally valid (!) status of *knowledge* (note!) of social life." At this point, the confusion between nomological regularity of the event and epistemic norm is obvious. The same holds for the conflation of "theoretical ground" and "existential ground." We find the same confusion at the top of page 16. Stammler claims that the "ultimate unity of social knowledge" is, on the one hand, "the fundamental *law* of all social life" and, on the other hand (a few lines later), the "universally valid foundation which makes possible the nomological *observation* of human social life." At this point, Stammler even succeeds in confusing the concepts of natural law, practical norm, and logical norm.

The careful reader is thereby pressed to the disagreeable conclusion that Stammler is not at all unaware of the ambiguity in his use of expressions like "nomological regularity" and "universal validity." Even the additions and deletions that distinguish the second edition from the first often seem calculated to strengthen this impression. In many cases, Stammler undoubtedly *knows* that his mode of expression is confusing and ambiguous. Consider this ambiguity of expression which we encounter repeatedly, an ambiguity of which Stammler can hardly be unaware. I want to make the following denial explicit and *as absolute as possible*: I am not raising a "moral" objection against Stammler on this score, not even in the most indirect sense imaginable. Just to the contrary. This ambiguity is a consequence of the idiosyncratic and instinctive "style" of the obstinate dogmatist and his belief in the "cosmic law" which is—or allegedly is—his original discovery. For the dogmatist, any inconsistency between his "dogma" and "science" is logically *impossible*. Like a sleepwalker, he moves with an absolute certainty of conviction, thereby evading the task of "strengthening" the weak points in his arguments by the elimination of ambiguity. Stammler leaves the confusion produced by his imprecise and ambiguous expressions securely in the hands of God. He is convinced that, somehow, the dubious issues will be resolved in conformity with the "law" he has discovered, and all will correspond to the order it entails. But suppose that we consider the matter from an unbiased point of view. Stammler begins his investigation with very modest conceptual tools. As we have seen in our examination of the first few pages of his book, he confuses even the most elementary categories in an utterly sophomoric fashion. Therefore it seems extremely improbable that Stammler could ever succeed in reaching any kind of understanding concerning what the theoretical goal of an "empirical" discipline can be and ought to be—for "social *science*," in *our* sense, is an "empirical" discipline.

Consider also the account of the logic of historical materialism parodied in the foregoing section. We are not concerned with the question of whether this account is an accurate exposition of historical materialism. However it is easy to understand how Stammler can accept this account and see it as refutable on one ground only: on the basis of *his* "theory of knowledge." Whoever conflates "laws of nature" and logical "norms" is a scholastic in the strictest sense of this word. Therefore he also finds scholastic logic irresistible. The fact that this is indeed the basis from which Stammler argues is established very clearly on page 19, where the general scientific status of historical materialism is described for the first time. In the second paragraph on p. 18, the *empirical* character of the problem seems to be explicitly acknowledged. The third paragraph follows with the claim that historical materialism attempts to set up a rigid "hierarchy" among the elements of social life. Apparently, therefore, its purpose is to establish the *causal* importance of these "elements" in their general, reciprocal relationships. A little earlier in the same paragraph, however, Stammler has just claimed that—given the standpoint of historical materialism—this point is a "methodological principle" of "*formal* significance." Then Stammler follows with another claim which, as usual, is confused. Given the "basic idea of the materialist conception of history" (see Stammler, the last line of p. 18 and also p. 19)—Stammler does not say whether this is an explicit thesis advocated by the representatives of historical materialism or whether he ascribes this thesis to them as a "consequence" of their position—it is necessary to make a *distinction* between "single laws which have been established" and "general, *formal* nomological regularity." "That is the definitive method for producing a correct synthesis of facts and laws."

As everyone knows, there is no expression more ambiguous than the word "formal" and no dichotomy more ambiguous than the distinction between form and content. The import of this distinction must be established with complete precision in *every* given case of its use. According to Stammler himself, the "basic idea" of historical materialism is the following: the nature and development of "economic phenomena" are invariably decisive in the formation of all other historical processes. In other words, economic "phenomena" constitute the unequivocal causes of all other historical phenomena. It is true that the imprecision of this concept of "economic phenomena" is objectionable. One point, however, is certain. This thesis is a substantive claim concerning the causal relationship which obtains between empirical events. Consider the claim that in a given *single case* or set of cases or in *types* of such cases—which may be more narrowly or extensively conceived—"economic" causes are decisive. The thesis in question can be distinguished from this latter claim *in one respect only*: by reference to its universality as a generalization. It is an hypothesis which one might attempt to "deduce" from the conditions of human life which actually obtain. Then the hypothesis could be verified "inductively" by comparing it with the "facts." However it remains a *substantive* hypothesis.

Suppose, for example, that someone claims that the theory of historical materialism is not to be conceived as a theoretical postulate, but rather as an "heuristic principle." And suppose that he attempts to set up a specific "method" for doing historical research "from an economic point of view." Obviously this makes absolutely no difference. Experience shows that in careful, dispassionate research there are circumstances under which this procedure can be extremely fruitful. But this is the case only if the general claim about the importance of economic conditions is treated as a substantive *hypothesis*, an hypothesis the import and limits of which are subject to empirical verification. It is absolutely impossible to change the general substantive import of this hypothesis so that it acquires a "formal" status. This hypothesis cannot be distinguished from "individual laws"—in other words, propositions of less comprehensive generality—as having a peculiarly *logical* import, an import in virtue of which the "validity" and the "scientific justification" of these "special laws" are *logically* "dependent" upon the hypothesis. Consider propositions which, at a given time, have the status of the ultimate ("highest") generalizations of a discipline, propositions like the law of the "conservation of energy." To describe these propositions as "formal" is obviously a matter of terminological preference. This description is often used because the "domain" of their validity is very extensive at the same time that their substantive "content" is very limited. But notice: It *cannot* be claimed that they have *no* substantive content. Every "higher" generalization can only be called "formal" in relation to "lower" generalizations: in other words, generalizations that are less comprehensive. All the "axioms" of physics are "ultimate" generalizations of this sort. That is, they are hypotheses of mathematical "self-evidence," and they have an extraordinarily high degree of empirical "conformation," a degree of confirmation that increases each time the hypothesis is used as an "heuristic principle." Nevertheless—and the debate on radioactivity shows this—the validity of these hypotheses remains dependent upon their "empirical confirmation." They are always subject to "empirical verification." Even a student in the first semester of logic is expected to know that these generalizations have not acquired the logical status of "formal," a priori principles of knowledge—the status of epistemological "categories." They can never occupy this status.

Suppose that someone like Stammler represents himself as an "epistemologist." And suppose that he makes it even more explicit that he bases his own views on Kant's. In that case, it is quite obvious that the same inexcusably juvenile error will ensue if he raises "axioms"—that is, propositions which "simplify" experience—to the status of "categories." The constitutive power of "categories" is a necessary condition for the "possibility" of any meaningful "experience." The same error is committed when these categories are described as empirical generalizations. Then, because we sometimes speak in an extremely imprecise fashion of the *"law* of causality," individual "natural laws" are viewed as "special cases" of the special conditions under which this "law" of causality "functions." And, corresponding to this error, the "law of causality" itself is viewed as the most comprehensive of all empirical generalizations. The last mistake is a retrogression beyond Kant to (at the very least) Hume. The first mistake, however, carries us much further back: in fact, all the way back to scholasticism.

Stammler's entire mode of argumentation is based on this relapse into a petrified scholasticism. To reread the parody offered above is eventually to be persuaded once more that it in fact corresponds both to the import of the passages quoted there and to the import of Stammler's remarks on pages 18 and 19 of his book. Consider the mistake which is the polar antithesis of the error of elevating empirical generalizations to the status of categories: namely, the conversion of categories into empirical propositions. It cannot be said that Stammler commits this error "explicitly." On the contrary, he wants to ground his theory of knowledge on the Kantian theory. Nevertheless, as we shall see shortly, this error is implicitly committed in his work. Later, when we examine the infirmity and the inconsistency of Stammler's discussion of the "question" of causality more closely, we shall be obliged to conclude that it makes very little practical difference whether "axioms" are elevated to the status of "categories" or "categories" demoted to the status of "axioms." Consider, finally, the elevation of purely *methodological* "rules" to the status of "formal principles" that are anchored on epistemological grounds. This is the best construction we can place upon Stammler's version of the "materialist conception of history," the account reproduced in the above parody. This error is the converse of the transposition of the basic principles of epistemology into "heuristic principles": that is, hypotheses that are subject to empirical verification. It is obvious that both errors are instances of the same mistake. And it is a self-proclaimed "neo"-Kantian who serves up all of this!

Finally, Stammler also represents "categories" as "problematics" "from which" generalizations follow (see Stammler, p. 12). This mistake is a patchwork of all the foregoing errors and other similar elementary logical mistakes. On p. 12, he explains that the following question is always essential. "Which uniform problematic" is to be employed in "generalizing from specific *observations* (note!)"? "The point of view of causality or *teleology*? And why one and not the other? In what sense can a detailed answer to this question be given?" First of all, suppose that this distinction can be made. There is no sense in which it constitutes a mutually exclusive dichotomy. The abstract concept "white objects," for example, is not constituted from the standpoint of "causality" or from the standpoint of "teleology." It is simply a logically articulated general idea, an elementary classificatory concept. Suppose we disregard this imprecision of expression. The question of the real import of this distinction still remains completely unresolved. What does it mean to "generalize from *observations* from the standpoint of teleology"?

At this point, we shall provide a brief account of the possible answers to this question. This account should be useful in some of our later discussions. Does this expression refer to the deductive inference of metaphysical "purposes of nature" from empirical "laws of nature"? Consider, for example, how Eduard von Hartmann attempts to employ the so-called "second law" of thermodynamics in order to demonstrate the ultimate "purpose" of the finite evolution of the cosmos. Or does the expression refer to the use of "teleological" concepts—for example, biological concepts—as heuristic principles in order to establish general insights into the relationships of organic phenomena? In the first case, the aim is to ground a metaphysical doctrine on empirical propositions. In the second case, the aim is to employ an "anthropomorphic" metaphysics for heuristic purposes in order to derive empirical propositions. Or should the empirical propositions be understood as generally "appropriate means" for the attainment of certain generally defined "purposes"? If so, then it is obvious that the issue simply concerns general, causal knowledge articulated in the logic of practical reasoning. Consider, for example, the following proposition. "In economic policy, the measure x can be used to produce the result y." This is only a transposition of the following empirical proposition, a proposition which expresses a general causal relation. "*Whenever* x takes place, then y is in general the *consequence*." This means: Either the consequence which invariably ensues or the consequence which "is to be expected."

Stammler could hardly accept the first of these three views. It is not his purpose to support a metaphysics, and least of all a naturalistic metaphysics. He would probably have to acknowledge that the other two cases are "generalizations in the causal sense." Or does he perhaps have in mind the logical analysis of general *value* judgments and moral or political postulates? Consider the proposition: "The protection of the weak is the duty of the state." Suppose we disregard the vagueness of the concepts of "protection" and "weakness." This proposition is a "general" *practical* maxim. Its truth content can obviously be discussed from the standpoint of its *axiological* validity. But it is obvious that the question of the axiological validity of this proposition is altogether different from the question of the confirmation of this proposition as an empirical fact or as a "law of nature." Does this proposition articulate a "generalization based on observation"? Or can a controversy concerning its truth content be resolved by "generalizations based on observation"?

In order to answer these questions, it is necessary to make a distinction. On the one hand, the controversy can concern the validity of an "imperative." In this case, the discussion of the maxim lies within the domain of ethical "norms." Or the controversy can concern the question of the de facto "applicability" of the maxim. In this case, the discussion concerns the third case just identified. The issue is to identify some item x which would have y (in this case: "protection of the weak") as its general consequence. The discussion would be concerned with the question: Is there a political measure which can be identified as this item x? This is a purely causal question concerning the applicability of "empirical generalizations." Or finally—and this is by far the most frequent case—no direct proof of the invalidity of the maxim is undertaken. It is claimed that the maxim cannot qualify as an imperative on the following grounds: its use inevitably leads to consequences which compromise the applicability of *other* maxims which do qualify as imperatives. In this case, the opponent of the maxim would undoubtedly attempt to establish empirical generalizations concerning the *consequences* of acting on this policy of social welfare: either by

direct induction or by hypotheses which are logical consequences of putatively established theses. In this case, the
purpose of the critic is to contest the "validity" of the
maxim by showing that its application is inconsistent with
the requirements of another "maxim": for example, the
maxim that it is the duty of the state to "preserve" the
physical health of the nation and to defend the bearers of
aesthetic and intellectual "culture" against "degeneration."
Naturally we are not concerned here with the manner in
which this maxim is formulated. Again, the empirical propositions which would be employed for this purpose fall under
the "third" case mentioned above. They are invariably general propositions which express causal relations, and their
logic may be articulated in the schema: y always, or as a
"rule," follows x.

But where are the generalizations from *observation* made
"on the basis of teleology," the *polar antitheses* of general
causal propositions? The two opposing maxims are *values*.
Ultimately, they must be "balanced" against one another,
and eventually it will be necessary to *choose* between them.
This choice certainly cannot be grounded on "generalizations" from "observation." On the contrary, it can only be
grounded on the "dialectical" investigation of the "immanent
consequences" of the two alternatives. In other words, it is
necessary to trace these maxims back to the "ultimate"
practical "axioms" on which they are based. As we shall see
in the ensuing, the deductions which Stammler undertakes in
the final chapter of his book represent just such a procedure.
And this is not the only context in which he emphasizes,
quite correctly, the absolute logical disparity between causal
"explanation" and "value judgment" and between prediction
and obligation. Even in the course of his exposition of
historical materialism, Stammler elucidates this dichotomy
(Stammler, pp. 51-55) in a "dialogue" between a "bour-
geois" and a "socialist," a dialogue that is remarkably percep-
tive and lucid. The two antagonists "are not fighting in the

same ring." This is because one antagonist is concerned with what—in view of (genuinely or allegedly) established generalizations—*will* inevitably take place. But the other is concerned with what—given certain (genuine or putative) cultural values—unconditionally *should* not take place. "It is," Stammler says, "the battle between the bear and the shark." Fine! In view of this, is it conceivable that a few pages later Stammler himself, quite in the same fashion that we have already encountered repeatedly, should treat these two completely independent problematics—and Stammler knows that they are different—as if they were *the same*? Or is this not the case on page 72, where Stammler raises the following question. "What, therefore, is the universally valid . . . procedure for generalizing (note!) from single *observations* (note!) of history and establishing them as 'nomological' phenomena?" Then, in exactly the same breath and without blinking an eye, he continues as follows. "Suppose that someone does not know what it means to *justify* (note!) a phenomenon of social life in general. In that case, it does not make sense to argue in a given instance whether or not a certain social attitude or aspiration is *justified* (note!)." Stammler himself does not know which ring he is fighting in. He thereby brings the "battle between the bear and the shark" to a conclusion by establishing a peaceful, temperate, and muddled coexistence between the two. Whoever does not see this, it seems to me, simply does not *want* to see it.

Page by page, we find Stammler constantly juggling with two heterogeneous problematics. In consequence, the reader is repeatedly mystified. However, as any reading of the book will show, this is far from being the most objectionable of the subterfuges and equivocations that Stammler employs in the "epistemological" substructure of his "critique" of historical materialism. At this point, suppose we consider the following problem. What does Stammler really *mean* by "social materialism." He uses this concept and the concept of the "materialist conception of history" interchangeably. Why are we justified in calling this "conception"—or, more accurately, the "conception" which is the (putative) object of Stammler's criticism—"materialist"? In spite of all the controversies among advocates of the "materialist conception of history," we would probably be justified in claiming that they all take the following position. This conception of history is "materialist" in two senses. It entails that "historical" processes are unequivocal consequences of the mode of the production and the appropriation of "material"—that is, economic—goods which prevails at any given time. And, in particular, it entails that man's "historical" conduct is unambiguously determined by his "material"—that is, economic—interests. Stammler quite willingly and repeatedly admits that *every* single concept employed in this definition—and in this context it is a purely provisional definition—raises problems. The import of these concepts is extremely imprecise. Perhaps it is not even possible to define them with absolute clarity. Perhaps they are intrinsically vague. Stammler also states explicitly that the distinction between "economic" and "noneconomic" determinants of events is invariably a product of *conceptual* analysis. Of course this is obvious to anyone who is familiar with the conditions under which scientific or scholarly work is possible.

However these admissions are quite inconsequential. Throughout his book Stammler conceives "economic" interests, "economic" phenomena, "material" relations, and so on as an objective component of the totality of "historical" or "cultural" phenomena. Above all—to use Stammler's jargon—he conceives them as a *component* of "societal life" or "social life." Stammler himself sees (Stammler, p. 18) that historical materialism is meant to entail some general view of the "hierarchical relationship" between *one* "element" of social life and *the other* "elements." In another passage (Stammler, pp. 64–67)—quite in agreement with the usual intent of this idiom—he cites some examples and provides a critical commentary on them, distinguishing the cases in which the functional causal relationship is concerned with "economic" ("material") motives from the cases in which it is concerned with non-"economic" motives. Three pages later, however, (Stammler, p. 70, see the penultimate paragraph) the following claim appears quite unexpectedly. "Suppose that the concept of the nomological regularity of social life is identified with the concept of the causal explanation of the process of social change. If this is the case, how can we resist the following conclusion: *ultimately, all* events of societal life which constitute objects of nomological knowledge are dependent upon (!) the socioeconomic base?"[7]

The *implications* of *this* argument are easy to see. It gives the historical materialist everything he needs, and more besides. How does Stammler propose to defend this argument? It is impossible to tell. Consider the proposition according to which there must be a causally sufficient condition for all historical events and every phenomenon of societal life. According to Stammler, it follows from this proposition that all historical events and every phenomenon of societal life must, in the final analysis, be explained *exclusively* by reference to *one* element of history or societal life. Any alternative would be inconsistent with the category of causality. But is there any reason to believe that this is the case? Stammler's account of this problem is quite incomprehensible. But wait! If we turn back two pages (Stammler, p. 68), we find the following claim: It is impossible to suppose that there is a plurality of "basic entities," entities in which "completely autonomous causal chains exist concomitantly." No intelligent student of history would ever make an assumption like that. On the contrary, everyone knows that in tracing the causal regress of every "individual phenomenon" we are led to an infinite number of questions. Consider "economic" phenomena—phenomena which arouse our *interest* and require explanation in a given case only because of their "economic aspects." The explanation of "economic" phenomena leads to political, religious, ethical, geographical, and other conditions. Why? For the same reason that the explanation of political phenomena leads to "economic" conditions, and also to every other sort of condition. Therefore the support which this proposition provides for his thesis is much more modest than Stammler himself supposes when he claims, immediately after stating the proposition, that any identification of a single "aspect"—presumably this point must also hold for economic "aspects"—for the purpose of a particular analysis only constitutes a conceptual abstraction from the "universal nexus."

Therefore the grounds for the sentiment which Stammler expresses on page 70 do not become any clearer. If we turn back one more page to the bottom of p. 67, however, we find the following claim. "Consider every single inquiry undertaken on the basis of the law of causality. A fundamental and necessary condition of any such inquiry is the assumption that all individual phenomena are exhaustively linked according to one (!) general law, a law which is exhibited (?) in each of the single phenomena." It is obvious that—at least as Stammler sees the matter—this is an epistemological axiom of historical materialism. The thesis of p. 70 that concerns us here is immediately intelligible if we regard it as a logical consequence of this axiom. Stammler regards both propositions as unconditional truths. How did Stammler reach this conclusion?

In view of the chaos generated by his book, certainty on a matter of this sort is not possible. However the conclusion seems to be a consequence of fallacies that have a variety of sources. First, Stammler apparently has the idea—and many related passages in his book confirm this—that the "exact" natural sciences employ the concept of the "reduction" of qualities to quantities: for example, the reduction of the qualities of light, sound, and heat to mechanical phenomena. The "ultimate" entities of the natural sciences are nonqualitative, material quantities. This has presumably led Stammler to the inference that only quantitative changes in matter are genuinely "real." 'Qualities" are merely the "subjective reflections" of matter in consciousness. Therefore they cannot qualify as "genuine realities." So, Stammler apparently concludes, given the theory of historical materialism, "matter" (economic relations and interests) and its "changes" constitute the exclusive realities of historical life. Everything else is only an ideological "superstructure," a "reflection" of "matter" and its "changes." Consider this analogy. It is radically mistaken and of no scientific value whatsoever. It is sufficiently well known that even now this analogy persists in dominating the thinking of some "historical materialists." It is obvious that our author must be numbered among them.

In addition, it appears that Stammler commits another fallacy that is just as commonplace as this one. It is a fallacy that we have already encountered. We are disposed to speak of a *"law"* of causality, employing this locution in expressions that are imprecise, and undoubtedly also directly misleading. Because of the manner in which we employ this form of words, the following move is all too easily made. The proposition that every event has a cause—at least in its use as a generalization—is conceived as the ultimate empirical generalization. It appears as the most abstract "theorem" of the empirical sciences. "Laws of nature," therefore, simply constitute "cases" or "exemplifications" of the validity of this theorem under different special "conditions." The "law of causality"—given this interpretation—has no implications of any sort concerning the concrete actuality of any possible world. But suppose that this law is "applied" to reality. Then one might easily be led to conclude that there must be *one fundamental* proposition the universal validity of which is absolute. It is a "general law" the substantive import of which must be the following: It is simply the *"law"* of causality insofar as it applies to and is valid for the *simplest* and the *most universal* "elements" of reality. Such a proposition would constitute a causal "cosmic law" of the sort that some adepts of naturalism fondly imagine. "In the final analysis," specific events that actually take place would only be instances of the "functioning" of the law under special conditions, in the same way that Kepler's laws of planetary motion might be conceived as an "instance" of the "functioning" of the law of universal gravitation.

Consider this conflation of laws of nature and "categories." This is, of course, an extremely embarrassing mistake for a neo-Kantian to make. Yet—as we established earlier—Stammler never commits this error explicitly. And if we attributed this view to him, he would very probably object. In which case, I pose a question. Suppose we consider the sheer nonsense that he has written in the two passages now under discussion (Stammler, the bottom of p. 67 and the penultimate paragraph of p. 70). Consider the relationship between these passages and a position of Stammler's that we have already encountered: the thesis according to which the most general theorem of a science must be a "formal" principle of that science. Suppose we also consider the relationship between these views and his constant confusion of "problematics" and "methodological principles," on the one hand, and transcendental (in the Kantian sense), and therefore a priori, "forms"—that is, *logical presuppositions* of experience—on the other. Unless we attribute the conflation of laws of nature and "categories" to Stammler, how is it possible to make any sense of these relationships?

However that may be, let us examine the proposition concerning the necessity of *a single* general law which must constitute the *uniform* problematic for the totality of *all* phenomena of social reality that are possible objects of causal explanation. And suppose we consider the relationship between this proposition and the following idea: this "ultimate" generalization is both a *"form"* of being and at the same time a *"form"* of the knowledge of social reality—social reality constituting the *"matter"* that corresponds to this *"form."* These propositions immediately generate paradoxical consequences. "Materialist" is an adjectival form of the noun "matter." Therefore it is possible to construct one "materialist" conception of history the essential feature of which is identified in the following proposition. The "form" of historical or "social" life—Stammler employs "historical" and "social" interchangeably without providing any further clarification—is determined by the "matter" of historical or "social" life. Of course it is obvious that—except for the use of the *word* "materialist"—this "conception" is completely irrelevant to what is generally understood by "historical materialism." And, as we have seen, Stammler repeatedly employs this generally received conception of historical materialism. Consider this *new* "conception" and the battery of concepts it requires. It is clear that *every* single "element" of "societal life" (we continue to speak Stammler's language)—including religion, politics, art, and science, and, of course, the "economy" too—is constituted from the same *matter*. Historical materialism, however, as this theory is usually understood and as it has been employed by Stammler up to this point, claims that all the other elements are dependent upon the "economy." Therefore the theory—as it is usually understood—makes a claim about the dependence of *one* part of this "matter" upon *another* part. But there is no sense in which it claims that the "form" of "social life"—in the new sense of this expression introduced by Stammler—is dependent upon its "matter."

Consider what is usually understood by the "materialist" conception of history. Versions of this theory sometimes contain claims like the following. Specific contradictions between political or religious ideas, and so on are "merely the *form*" in which "material conflicts of interest" *are expressed*. Also the phenomena of light, heat, electricity, magnetism, and so on are sometimes described as different "forms" of "energy." But it is obvious that in these two contexts the *import* of the expression "form" is *precisely the contrary* of the *import* of the expression "formal" as Stammler employs it in his arguments. In Stammler's arguments, "form" is employed to designate homogeneity, generality, and "fundamental universality," in contrast to the heterogeneity and multiplicity of "content." But in these two contexts, "form" refers to the transitory and heterogeneous features of "phenomena," features which conceal the unity of genuine reality. Therefore the transitory "forms"—as understood by the materialist conception of history—are precisely what Stammler calls "matter." This shows how dangerous it is to employ categories like "form" and "content" without supplying a completely unambiguous analysis of this distinction. But of course ambiguity is the definitive feature of Stammler's style. It is only this element of ambiguity which makes it possible for Stammler to employ his scholastic equipment to fish in conceptually "troubled waters."

Straightaway, Stammler begins to juggle with these two radically different concepts of "materialist." It is only this trick which opens the following possibilities of confusion. On page 37, Stammler describes the dependence of religion and morals, art and science, social ideas, and so on upon *economic life*. Arguing along the same lines on page 64, *seq.*, he considers the question of the *economic* causes of the Crusades and the reception of Roman law. He also considers the question of the *political* causes of the development of peasant holdings in land. These issues are described as cases which confirm the validity of the materialist conception of history. On p. 132, however, "*collective* human action based upon need satisfaction" (on p. 136, Stammler defines "need satisfaction" as "the production of pleasure and the avoidance of pain") is simply described as "matter." The "empirical events of human life, *without any exception at all*, are *based on*" this material foundation (Stammler, p. 136, penultimate paragraph). Stammler repudiates most decisively the possibility of establishing distinctions within this "matter," distinctions based on the "kinds" of needs to be satisfied (Stammler, p. 138) and (insofar as only "collective action" is at stake) the means to be employed for the satisfaction of these needs (Stammler, p. 140). *Then* Stammler has the presumption to employ *this latter* conception of the "material" properties of social life (in contrast to their "*formal*" properties) in order to "refute" historical materialism—an historical materialism which employs a completely *different* concept of the "material" properties of social life (the principal purpose of the historical materialist concept is to establish a distinction between the "material" and the "ideological"). But there is another point which we have not yet covered.

In his remarks on page 132, and following, which we mentioned for the purpose of illustration, Stammler has already introduced a more precise account of the distinction between form and content. In his view, the validity of this particular dichotomy is a peculiar feature of "social life." It is a constitutive property of the concept of "social life." After so much criticism of Stammler's preliminary discussions, let us turn to this dichotomy, the real essence of Stammler's theory. In response to the foregoing criticism we can imagine the following reply from Stammler or from one of his disciples. "Why does my book mystify you? Because you take it seriously! By necessity, I began the book by speaking the conceptual language of historical materialism. But my purpose is to show that this conceptual language produces absurdities. I show how the speaker of this language is suffocated by the morass of confusion in which this language traps him Read on. You will discover both the immanent refutation of this conception and, at the same time, its replacement by a new, purified theory. In the early part of the book, I, your prophet, have—so to speak—only pretended to be a wolf in sheep's clothing."

Of course the quality of this imitation—if, indeed, it is an imitation—is very dubious. Nevertheless we ought to consider the possibility that it is Stammler himself who has mystified us up to this point. He invariably evades the clarification of the points at which he no longer speaks with the voice of the historical materialist, the points at which he begins to speak for himself. Moreover he concludes Book One of his work—the only part of the work that we have thus far subjected to a limited analysis—with a reference to what awaits us, promising "truths that have never been uttered before," a remark that is completely serious in its solemnity. Therefore on to Book Two. Let us have a look at the profusion of gifts it has to offer. However it will be useful if we keep the following in mind: the doubts created by the foregoing analysis and the manner in which Stammler—doutblessly speaking for himself and *not* as a proxy for the historical materialist—fails to distinguish fundamentally different categories of knowledge.

The explicit purpose of Stammler's work is to prove that an absolute, definitive distinction must be made between the "science of social life" and the "natural sciences." This proof is undertaken by showing that "social life," as an *object* of investigation, is completely different from "nature." Therefore it is logically necessary to set forth a principle of investigation in the social sciences that is different from the "method" of the natural sciences. These dichotomies are obviously meant to be mutually *exclusive*. So it is of the utmost importance to have an unambiguous account of what is meant by "nature," the "natural sciences," and the "scientific method." What is the definitive criterion for the identification of "nature," the "natural sciences," and the "scientific method"? The methodological discussions published during the last few years clearly establish that the answer to this question is certainly not self-evident. Stammler, of course, either does not know this literature at all or is only superficially acquainted with it. At the outset, let us admit that quite often we all use the expressions "nature" and "natural scientific" with careless imprecision, assuming that their import will be clear in any concrete case. This can be a dangerous way of proceeding. Consider, moreover, Stammler's predicament. His entire doctrine is based on an absolutely strict and mutually exclusive conceptual distinction between the objects "nature" and "social life." Therefore at least some reflection concerning *what* is to be understood by "nature" is of critical importance to Stammler's enterprise.

In ordinary discourse, the word "nature" is used in several ways. (1) Sometimes it refers to "inanimate" nature. (2) Or sometimes it refers both to "inanimate" nature and to all "organic" phenomena that are not distinctively human. (3) Or sometimes it refers to both these objects and, in addition, to those organic characteristics of a "vegetative" or "animal" sort which men and animals share. In this third sense of the word, therefore, it is the so-called "higher," "intellectual" or "spiritual" functions that are excluded from the domain of nature, functions that are peculiarly human. Therefore— although a significant margin of imprecision is unavoidable in this context—the limits of the concept of "nature" may be defined approximately as follows. In sense (1), the objects which physiology (plant and animal physiology) defines as its subject matter within the totality of the empirically given lie outside the domain of nature. In sense (2), it is the subject matter of psychology (both animal *and* human psychology) that lies outside the domain of nature. And in sense (3), it is the subject matter of those empirical disciplines which investigate "cultural phenomena" (ethnology and "cultural history," in the most extensive sense of these terms) that lies outside the domain of nature. In each of these three senses, however, nature is invariably conceived as a complex of certain kinds of *objects*, a complex that is distinguished from another complex of *objects* which have different properties.

Now consider another distinction. It entails a concept of "nature" the *logical* properties of which are different from the *logical* properties of this more colloquial concept. The investigation of empirical reality in the interest of establishing "abstractions"—timelessly valid empirical generalizations ("laws of nature")—may be identified as "natural science" and distinguished from the investigation of the same empirical reality in the interest of establishing the causal conditions for the existence of the "concrete individual entity." In this case, the distinction is based on the *kind* of question posed by the investigation. The antithesis of "nature," therefore, is "history." Given this distinction, disciplines like "psychology," "social psychology," "sociology," theoretical socioeconomics, "comparative religion," and "comparative jurisprudence" all fall within the domain of the natural sciences. Dogmatic or prescriptive disciplines are not covered by this distinction at all.

Finally,[8] a third concept of "natural science"—and, by implication, also a third concept of "nature"—is a consequence of the following distinction. On the one hand, consider all those disciplines which attempt to establish empirical-causal "explanations." On the other hand, consider those disciplines in which the results are dogmatic—either normatively or logically prescriptive. Logic, ethical theory and aesthetics, mathematics, jurisprudence conceived as a prescriptive or dogmatical discipline, and metaphysical (for example, theological) dogmatics fall into the latter collection of disciplines. In this case, the distinction is based on the logical properties of the propositions with which the discipline is concerned. "Existential" propositions are to be distinguished from "prescriptive" or "axiological" propositions. Given this distinction, the subject matter of all the "historical sciences"—including, for example, the history of art, the history of ethics, economic and legal history—is included in the domain of "natural science." In this sense of "nature," "natural science" comprehends every investigation which employs the category of causality.

In the ensuing, we shall explore two further possible concepts of "nature." For the present, we shall suspend this particular analysis. The ambiguity of the concept of "nature" is obvious enough. In view of this ambiguity, we shall always have to consider what *Stammler* means by "nature" when he discusses the distinction between "social life" and "nature." At this point, however, let us take up the following question.

What are the constitutive properties of the polar antithesis of "nature" that Stammler has discovered? In other words: Under what conditions does any item fall within the domain of "social life"? It is on the basis of this concept of "social life" that Stammler constructs his entire argument.

Analysis of the Concept of a Rule: The Concepts of Regularity, Norm, and Maxim

According to Stammler, the distinguishing feature of "social life"—its "formally" definitive property—is the fact that it is *"rule-governed"* collective life. It is a collective life constituted by reciprocal relationships "between publicly observable rules." Before we follow Stammler's discussion any further, suppose we pause to consider the following question. What are the possible referents of the expressions "rule" and "rule-governed"? (1) "Rules" can be understood as general propositions concerning *causal* relationships: "laws of nature." Suppose we include in the class of "laws" only general propositions of unconditional rigor (rigor in the sense of unconditional universality). (a) Then the expression "rule" can be reserved exclusivel, for all empirical generalizations which do not have this status of unconditional universality. (b) The expression "rule" can also be reserved for all those so-called "empirical laws" which satisfy the following condition: although the "empirical law" in question is empirically and unconditionally universal, there is no knowledge, or no theoretically satisfactory knowledge, of the causal conditions responsible for its universality. In sense (1b) it is a "rule"—an "empirical law"—that man is "mortal." In sense (1a) it is a "rule"—an empirical generalization—that a box on the ears is "sufficient" to produce certain reactions of a specific nature on the part of the fraternity student for whom it is intended. (2) A "rule" can also be understood as a "norm," a *value* judgment which serves as a standard by reference to which present, past, or future events are "measured." Therefore it is the expression of a (logical, ethical, or aesthetic) *prescription*. It does not state a matter of fact concerning empirical "existence," the exclusive concern of "rules" in senses (1a) and (1b). The "validity" of the rule in sense (2) is constituted by a general imperative.[9] The content of this imperative is the norm itself. In sense (1), the "validity" of the rule is simply constituted by the putative "validity" of the claim that the corresponding factual regularities expressed by the rule are either "given" in empirical reality or can be inferred from empirical reality by generalization.

The import of these two fundamental meanings of "rule" and the "rule-governed" is quite simple. However these concepts have other meanings that do not seem to fit smoothly into either of these two senses. One of these is the sort of rule that is usually called a "maxim" of conduct. Consider, for example, the case of Defoe's Robinson Crusoe. In his use of Robinson, Stammler follows economic theory. In the ensuing, therefore, we shall be obliged to do the same. In his isolation, Robinson manages a "rational" *economy* that is suited to the circumstances of his existence. This undoubtedly means the following: in the production and consumption of goods, he imposes certain "rules" upon his conduct, "economic" rules in particular. Consider, therefore, the supposition according to which there are *conceptual* reasons why the economic "rule" presupposes a plurality of agents associated by and subject to the rule. This assumption is mistaken.[10] At least this follows if the case of Robinson can be used to prove anything. Robinson, of course, is an imaginary product of literary art, a mere conceptual construct which the "scholastic" manipulates. But Stammler is a scholastic himself. Therefore it surely must have occurred to him that his readers would use Robinson in the same way he does. In addition, consider the following. This issue concerns a rigorous "conceptual" definition. Stammler regards the concept of a "rule" as *logically* constitutive for "social" life. Moreover he thinks that "economic phenomena" are "conceptually" possible only within the domain of "social rules." In view of this, consider the status of an artificial construct like Robinson, a construct that satisfies the following conditions: it is both internally consistent from a "logical" point of view and—this is not the same as internal consistency—it is also consistent with every "possibility" entailed by empirical generalizations. A fabricated construct of this sort is irrelevant to the "concept" of a rule.

In addition, Stammler makes a very serious mistake when he attempts to avoid this argument with the following claim (Stammler, p. 84): Robinson is *causally* conceivable only as a product of the "social life" from which, by chance, he has disappeared as a castaway. Stammler himself has sermonized on this point: The question of the causal genesis of a "rule" is completely irrelevant to the question of its conceptual status. This point is quite correct, but it certainly does not strengthen Stammler's case in the present context. Stammler also claims (Stammler, p. 146 and many other passages) that an isolated conceptual construct of this sort can be explained by "natural science." This is because the case of Robinson Crusoe is only concerned with "nature and the technological (note!) mastery of nature." But recall the systematic ambiguity of the concepts of "nature" and "natural science" discussed above. *Which* of the various concepts of "nature" and "natural science" does Stammler have in mind at this point? And if we are exclusively concerned with the concept of a "rule," the following point is most important: "technique" is a process governed by "rules" that are "purposefully instituted." Consider the parts of a machine. They function according to "humanly instituted rules." Draught horses or slaves forcibly harnessed together—or, finally, the "free" wage laborers in a factory—function according to "humanly instituted rules" in precisely the same "logical" sense. In the last case it is calculated *"psychological* pressure," properly applied, that harnesses the worker to the total mechanism. This "pressure" is occasioned by the "idea" of the empty pocketbook and the hungry family, and so on which would follow the disruption of the regular "order of work" and its consequence, the closing of the factory. Perhaps it is also occasioned by all sorts of other ideas—ethical ideas, for example. Finally, it may be a consequence of mere "habit." In the case of the parts of the machine, it is their physical and chemical properties that lock them into the total mechanism. But this difference is obviously of no consequence at all for the *import* of the concept of a "rule" as it applies to these two cases.

Consider the following ideas in the mind of the "wage laborer." In view of his experiential knowledge, he sees the satisfaction of his needs for food, clothing, and housing as "dependent upon" the following fact: while he is "on the job," he utters certain formulae or produces other tokens that are customary requirements of the sort of document a "lawyer" would call a "labor contract." If he physically adapts himself to certain mechanisms, and therefore performs certain motor activities, he sees that he has the opportunity to receive periodically certain characteristically shaped metal disks or slips of paper. If he places these in the hands of other people, it will follow that he can acquire bread, trousers, and so on. In fact, should someone attempt to deprive him of these objects, there is a certain probability that people with spiked helmets would respond to his call and help him get them back. This is an extremely complicated series of reflections, and here it is only sketched in the crudest possible fashion. The presence of these ideas in the minds of the workers can be counted upon with a certain degree of probability. The manufacturer takes these ideas into account as causally decisive factors which determine how labor power functions in the technical process of production. He depends upon these factors in the same way that he takes account of the weight, tensile strength, elasticity, and other physical properties of the raw material on which his machinery works or the physical properties of the machinery itself. Both the ideas of his workers and the physical properties of the raw material and the machinery constitute, in exactly the same *logical* sense, causal conditions of a certain "technical" result—for example, the production of x tons of pig iron from y tons of ore within the timespan z. The fact that both processes "function according to *rules*" is a "precondition"— in exactly the same *logical* sense—for the technical result. In the one case, "processes of consciousness" are included in the causal chain. In the other case, they are not. But from a *"logical"* point of view, this difference is of absolutely no consequence.

Consider, therefore, Stammler's distinction between the problematics of "technique" and "social science." He claims that a "socioscientific" inquiry is concerned with phenomena which "function according to rules." But this is not a criterion which is sufficient to establish a conclusive or definitive difference between these two problematics. The hunter counts on the qualities of his dog. In exactly the same way, the manufacturer takes the following facts into account in his calculations. There are hungry people on the scene. However other people with spiked helmets prevent them from using physical force in order to take food wherever they happen to find it. Therefore the complex series of reflections sketched above must take place. The hunter counts on the fact that his dog will respond to his whistle in a certain way or will perform certain tasks after he hears a shot. In exactly the same fashion, the manufacturer counts on the following fact: If a paper printed in a certain way ("regulations of work") is posted, a certain result will be more or less assured.

Consider another example. The "economic" behavior of Robinson Crusoe in relation to the "supplies of goods" and means of production available on his island corresponds to the fashion in which the contemporary person employs those little metal disks that are called "money." Suppose that he has these disks in his pocket. Or suppose that, on the basis of founded or unfounded beliefs, he thinks he has the chance to acquire these disks by making the right moves (for example, by scribbling certain marks on a piece of paper called a "check" or clipping another slip of paper called a "coupon" and showing it to another person behind a certain counter). He knows that if these disks are employed in a certain fashion, he can as a matter of fact acquire certain objects that he has seen behind glass windows, on restaurant buffets, and in other places. He knows—either through personal experience or through instruction—that if he simply takes these objects without further ado, the people with the spiked helmets will appear and put him behind bars. How did it really come about that these little metal disks developed these remarkable potentialities? The modern individual does not need to know the answer to this question, no more than he needs to know how his legs make it possible for him to walk. He can be content with the following observation, made from childhood: Money regularly functions in the same way regardless of the person who uses it. This observation has the same status as the following propositions. At least in general, anyone who has legs can walk. A stove that has been fired produces heat. It is warmer in July than in April. The manner in which the modern individual uses money is based on his knowledge of the "nature" of money. He *"regulates"* his use of money and thereby "economizes."

Consider the following problems. *How* is this regulation in fact undertaken by a concrete individual? In this respect, he behaves like thousands and millions of other individuals: on the basis of his "experiences" or on the basis of what he has learned about the "consequences" of different possible ways of "regulating" the spending of money. How is it that this "regulation" will have the following consequence: members of different identifiable groups in a given population will, as a result of the allotment of opportunities, have *different* amounts of these metal disks (or the equally "effective" slips of paper) at their disposal? According to Stammler, the consideration and—insofar as the disposition of the data makes this possible—the solution to these problems must lie within the domain of the sciences of *nature* and "technique" and *not* within the domain of the "social sciences." That is because these questions concern the explanation of the behavior of a *single* individual. Both the "rules" employed by the modern individual just discussed and the "rules" employed by Robinson Crusoe are "maxims" in exactly the same sense. In both cases, the causal efficacy of the "maxim" for the empirical conduct of the individual is based on empirical generalizations which he has either discovered for himself or learned from others. The logic of these generalizations may be articulated as follows: if I do x, then, according to empirical generalizations, y will follow. The "rule-governed, purposive conduct" of Robinson is based on "experiential propositions" of this sort. Precisely the same holds for the conduct of those who "possess money." The existential conditions with which the latter has to "reckon"—in comparison with the conditions which Robinson must take into account—may be enormously complex. From a *logical* point of view, however, there is no difference between the two cases.

Both Robinson and the possessor of money are obliged to make calculations of the following sort. Given a certain action on my part, what empirically confirmed responses can be expected from "objective reality"? In one case, "objective reality" includes the reactions of human beings. In the case of Robinson Crusoe, it includes only the reactions of animals, plants, and "inanimate" natural objects. However this difference is of no consequence at all for the "*logical*" status of the "maxim" in question. Is Robinson's "economic behavior," as Stammler claims, "exclusively" a matter of technique *and therefore* not a possible object of "social science"? If this is the case, then the same holds for the conduct of the individual in relation to any plurality of human beings, regardless of how this plurality is constituted. That is to say, the same holds for this individual insofar as the investigation is concerned with the "regulation" of his conduct by "economic" maxims and the efficacy of these maxims. This point may be expressed in the language of ordinary discourse by saying that the "private economy" of the single individual is governed by "maxims." In Stammler's jargon, these maxims fall within the domain of "technique." They "regulate" the conduct of the individual with a consistency that is subject to empirical variations. In view of what he says about the case of Robinson, however, these maxims cannot be equivalent to "rules" as Stammler conceives them. Before we examine Stammler's concept of "rule" more closely, suppose we take up the following question. How is the concept of a "maxim " which we have used so freely, related to the two "types" of the concept of a "rule" identified in the foregoing discussion: "empirical regularity or uniformity" and "norm"? The answer to this question requires an additional, brief, general discussion of the following problem: What does it mean to say that a certain action is "rule-governed"?

Consider the proposition "my digestion is rule-governed." Most obviously, this proposition merely states the following simple "fact of nature": the process of digestion transpires within a certain temporal sequence. The "rule" is an abstraction from the natural process. However it can be transposed into an expression of necessity which "regulates" the process of digestion by eliminating sources of "disorder." In both cases the proposition which expresses the rule and the process that is said to be regulated may be exactly the same. But the import of the concept "rule" in these two cases is not the same. In the first case, the "rule" expresses an *observation* concerning the course of "nature." In the second case, it expresses a *goal* for which "nature" *strives*. Of course observational and teleological "regularities" can in fact coincide, a very happy consequence whenever it happens. However the "conceptual" import of these two regularities is not the same. The first is an empirical fact. The second is the object of an aspiration, an ideal, or a "norm" by reference to which the facts are "evaluated." The rule as "ideal" can play a role in two different kinds of investigation. One kind is concerned with the problem: What *empirical* regularity *would* correspond to the "ideal" in question? The other kind is concerned with the question: What state of *empirical* regularity is a causal consequence of the attempt to achieve the "ideal"?

Consider, by way of example, someone who employs the norms of hygiene as "standards" and "regulates" his conduct in accordance with these norms. This fact is *one* of the causal components responsible for the empirical regularities that can be observed in his physiology. These empirical regularities are causally influenced by innumerable conditions. And *among* these conditions is the medication the person uses in order to "realize" the hygienic "norm." As we see, his empirical "maxim" is the idea of the "norm." It is a real, effective agent, causally responsible for his action. Precisely the same points hold concerning the sense in which human conduct is "rule-governed" in relation to economic goods and other men—especially in relation to their "economic" behavior. Consider the illustrations of Robinson and the possessor of money discussed in the foregoing. Their behavior in relation to their economic goods—money, for example—appears to be "regulated." This fact can lead us to provide a theoretical formulation of the "rule" which we see, at least in part, as "governing" their behavior: a "principle of marginal utility," for example. This *ideal* "rule" entails a proposition concerning the content of the "norm" which Robinson "must have" followed *if* he intended to act in accordance with the ideal of "purposive" action. On the one hand, this *ideal* "rule" can be conceived as a standard of evaluation. It is obviously not a "moral" standard. It is a "teleological" standard which presupposes "purposive" conduct as an "ideal." On the other hand and more interestingly, this *ideal* "rule" is an heuristic principle. Let us assume that a person like Robinson Crusoe really exists. This heuristic principle can be employed to discover the actual causal conditions for his empirical conduct. In this case, the *ideal* "rule" serves as an "idealtypical" construction. We employ it as an hypothesis which must be "verified" in order to determine whether it agrees with the "facts." Such an "idealtypical" construction may prove to be useful in answering the following question. What are the *empirical* causes responsible for the person's conduct, and to what extent does his conduct approximate its "idealtypical" representation?[11]

This sort of "rule" of purposive action is germane to *empirical* knowledge of Robinson's behavior in two very different senses. On the one hand, it may possibly function as one of Robinson's "maxims," the "maxims" which constitute the *subject matter* of the investigation. In this case, the "rule" identifies a real "cause" of his actual conduct. On the other hand, this sort of "rule" may function as a component of the theoretical and conceptual apparatus employed by the *investigator*. His knowledge of the ideally possible "meaning" of the action makes it possible for him to acquire empirical knowledge of its real properties. A strict distinction must be made between these two senses of "rule." Within the domain of the empirical, the "norm" is undoubtedly a determinant of events. But it is only *one* determinant. From a logical point of view it qualifies as *one* determinant of events in the same sense that the "normative" use of medication—and therefore the "norm" which the doctor prescribes—constitutes one, but only one, of the determinants of the "regulation" of digestion which is the actual consequence of acting on this "norm". These determinants can influence conduct with very different degrees of *consciousness*.

Consider the child who "learns" how to walk, to keep himself clean, and to shun unhygienic pleasures. He sees that the life of other people proceeds according to certain "rules." By "learning" to do these things, he internalizes these "rules." He learns how to "express" himself in a language, and he learns how to behave "with civility." (1) *In part* he does all this without consciously formulating the rule which he—with very different degrees of consistency—in fact follows. (2) *In part* he does this on the basis of the conscious application of "empirical propositions" of the type: y is a consequence of x. (3) And *in part* he does it because—whether through "education" or through simple imitation—the "rule" has been impressed upon him as the idea of an intrinsically *obligatory* "norm" the fulfillment of which is good for its own sake. This "norm" is continually influenced by his own reflections and "experiences of life." As such, it constitutes a causal determinant of his conduct. Consider cases (2) and (3). Suppose it is claimed that in these cases a given moral, conventional, or teleological rule constitutes the *"cause"* of a given action. It is obvious that this is an extremely imprecise way of expressing the matter. The cause of the action in question is not the "ideal validity" of the norm, but rather the actual empirical idea of the actor who believes that the norm "should validly apply to" his conduct. This point holds for "ethical" norms just as it does for rules the "putative validity" of which is purely a "matter of convention" or "prudence." For example, it is obviously not the conventional rule of greeting that tips my hat when I meet an acquaintance. On the contrary, my hand does it. But what is causally responsible for this? I may merely be in the "habit" of following such a "rule." In addition, I may know from experience that my acquaintance would regard my failure to greet him as a lapse of propriety. The result would be unpleasant. In this case, therefore, the action is a consequence of a "utilitarian" calculation. Or, finally, I may act on the belief that it is "not proper" for me to disregard a harmless "conventional rule" that is universally observed unless there is some compelling reason to do so. Therefore I act on the basis of my "idea of a norm."[12]

The discussion of these last few examples brings us to the concept of a *"social* rule": that is, a rule which is "valid for" human relationships. This is the concept in which Stammler anchors the object "social life." We shall defer the question of the justification of Stammler's definition of this concept. For the present, let us pursue our discussion of the concept of a "rule"—independent of any consideration of Stammler's views—somewhat further.

First let us consider an elementary example. Stammler also uses this example occasionally in order to clarify the significance of the concept of a "rule" for the concept of "social life." Let us suppose that two men who otherwise engage in no "social relation"—for example, two uncivilized men of different races, or a European who encounters a native in darkest Africa—meet and "exchange" two objects. We are inclined to think that a mere description of what can be observed during this exchange—muscular movements and, if some words were "spoken," the sounds which, so to say, constitute the "matter" or "material" of the behavior—would in no sense comprehend the "essence" of what happens. This is quite correct. The "essence" of what happens is constituted by the "meaning" which the two parties ascribe to their observable behavior, a "meaning" which "regulates" the course of their future conduct. Without this "meaning," we are inclined to say, an "exchange" is neither empirically possible nor conceptually imaginable. Of course! The fact that "observable" signs function as "symbols" is one of the constitutive presuppositions of all "social" relations. But consider the following question: Is this presupposition *peculiar* to "social" relations?

It is obvious that there is no sense in which this is the case. Suppose I put a "bookmark" in a "book." It is obvious that the "publicly" observable results of this action only constitute a "symbol." This "symbol" is a sign of the fact that a slip of paper or another object placed between two pages has a "meaning." Independent of the knowledge of this meaning, the bookmark is both useless and meaningless for me. In addition, the act of placing it between the pages of a book would remain causally "inexplicable." But notice that no "social" relation of any sort is established in this case. The same point can be made concerning the conduct of Robinson Crusoe on his island. Suppose that Robinson, in the interest of managing the reforestation of his island "economically," "marks" certain trees which he intends to cut for the coming winter with an ax. Or suppose that he "economizes" with his corn supplies, rationing them and storing away one portion to serve especially as "seed corn." In all such cases—and in numerous other similar cases which the reader can construct for himself—the "publicly" observable event is certainly not "the entire event." The definitive properties and the "significance" of these measures are a consequence of their "meaning." But it is quite certain that the use of these measures does not imply the existence of any "social life." In principle, precisely the same point holds in the following relationships: the relationship between the "phonetic meaning" of the little black marks "printed" in a file of papers and the publicly observable aspects of these marks; the relationship between the "semantic meaning" of the sounds which another person "speaks" and the publicly observable aspects of these sounds; and, finally, the relationship between the "meaning" which each of the two parties to the exchange associates with his conduct and the publicly observable aspects of their conduct.

Suppose that for conceptual purposes we distinguish the "meaning" which we find "expressed" in an object or process from all the other components of the object or process which remain after this "meaning" is abstracted from it. And suppose that we define the sort of inquiry that is *exclusively* concerned with this last set of components as "naturalistic." The result is still another concept of "nature." It can be differentiated from the concepts of "nature" identified in our earlier discussion. In this sense of "nature," nature is the domain of the "meaningless." Or, more precisely, an item *becomes* a part of "nature" *if* we cannot raise the question: What is its "meaning"? Therefore it is self-evident that the polar antithesis of "nature" as the "meaningless" is not "social life," but rather the "meaningful": that is, the "meaning" ascribed to a process or object, the "meaning" which *can* "be found in it." This includes, at one extreme, the metaphysical "meaning" of the cosmos as seen from the perspective of a certain system of religious dogmatics. At another extreme, it includes the "meaning" which the barking of Robinson Crusoe's dog "has" when a wolf approaches. Therefore we have shown that there is no sense in which the property of being "meaningful"—the property of "meaning" or "signifying" something—is a feature peculiar to "social" life, its definitive property.

At this point let us return to the process of "exchange" discussed above. The "meaning" of the "observable" behavior of the two parties to the exchange can be conceived in two ways. From a logical point of view, these conceptions are very different. On the one hand, "meaning" can be conceived as *"idea."* We can raise the following questions. What *logical* or *conceptual* consequences can be identified in the "meaning" which *"we"*—the observers—ascribe to a concrete process of this sort? How can this "meaning" be included within a more comprehensive ideational system of "meaning"? From the "perspective" of such an investigation of "meaning," we could then undertake to "evaluate" the actual development of the process. For example, we could ask: What "must" the "economic" behavior of Robinson have been if it had been pursued to its ultimate conceptual or logical consequences? This is the sort of question raised by marginal utility theory. Then we could use this standard—a product of conceptual analysis—as a way of determining how his actual conduct "measures up." In quite the same way, we could ask: following the observed completion of the act of exchanging the objects, how "must" the two "exchange partners" behave if their conduct is to correspond to the "idea" of the exchange? In other words, suppose that their subsequent behavior conformed to the logical consequences of the "meaning" which *we* ascribe to their conduct. If this were the case, how would they have to behave? Therefore we begin with the following empirical fact. Processes of a certain sort have *in fact* taken place. A certain "meaning" is ideationally associated with these processes. It is not a "meaning" which has been analyzed clearly and distinctly, but rather a "meaning" which is only vaguely associated with these processes. Then, however, we *abandon* the domain of the empirical and pose the following question: How must the "meaning" of the conduct of the actors be *conceptually* construed in order to produce an internally consistent conceptual construct of that "meaning"?[13] In other words, we are engaged in what could be called a "dogmatics" of "meaning." On the other hand, we could pose the following questions. Consider the "meaning" which "we" could dogmatically or prescriptively ascribe to a process of this sort. Was it also the "meaning" which each of the actual participants in this process consciously ascribed to it? Or did each of the participants ascribe some other "meaning" to this process? Did they consciously ascribe any "meaning" at all to the process?

It follows that we are obliged to distinguish two different "meanings" of the concept of "meaning" itself. Both are *empirical* concepts of "meaning," the only sense of the concept that concerns us now. In our example, the "meaning" of the act of exchange might be the following. The actors consciously *intended to* impose an "obligatory" *norm* upon their conduct. Therefore they had the (subjective) intention that their conduct should be obligatory because it should conform to this *norm*. In other words, they may have established a "normative maxim."[14] On the other hand, the "meaning" of the act of exchange might be the following. Each of the parties participates in the exchange in order to achieve a certain "result." In view of his "experience," each sees his action as a "means" for achieving this result. The exchange, therefore, has a (subjectively) intended "purpose."

It is obvious that in any given case the extent to which either of the two sorts of maxims can be empirically identified is problematical. In the case of the "normative maxim," moreover, there is the question of whether it can be empirically identified *at all*. The relevant questions here are the following. (1) To what extent were the two exchange partners in our example really aware of the "utilitarian" character of their conduct? (2) On the other hand, to what extent did the two exchange partners act on the idea that their relationship *"should"* be "regulated" in such a way that the two objects of the exchange qualify as "equivalent"? To what extent did they consciously adopt the following "normative maxim": each partner *should* "respect the new ownership" which the exchange creates in the object that was formerly his own possession? As regards question (2), the relevant issues are the following. (a) To what extent was the idea of this "meaning" a causal determinant of the decision to participate in this particular "act of exchange"? (b) To what extent did the idea of this "meaning" constitute the basic determinant of their conduct *subsequent to* the exchange?

Consider *our* "dogmatic" conceptual construct of the "meaning" of the "exchange." It is a "heuristic principle" for framing hypotheses. It is obvious that this construct will be very useful in answering these questions. On the other hand, it is also obvious that the following elementary precept must be kept in mind. There is no sense in which this conceptual construct would "objectively" establish the "meaning" of the exchange. A definitive "meaning" of this sort is "possible" only if it could be dogmatically deduced from a given set of logical principles. Suppose it were simply decreed that the two exchange partners *meant* to "regulate" their social relations so that they would correspond to the ideal "concept" of an "exchange." On what grounds? Because we, the observers, on the basis of our *dogmatic* classification, ascribe this "meaning" to their conduct. It is obvious that this would be a pure fiction, corresponding to the reification of the "regulative idea" of the "social contract" or "civil compact." From a logical point of view, the following proposition has the same status. In view of the "meaning" which its barking can have for its *owner*, the dog barks because it "wants" to realize the "idea" of protection of private property. From an empirical point of view, the dogmatic "meaning" of the "exchange" is an "idealtype." A vast number of processes which occur in empirical reality correspond to this "idealtype" with varying degrees of "exactitude." For this reason, we use the "idealtype" for both "heuristic" and "taxonomical" purposes. "Normative" maxims which treat this "ideal" meaning of the exchange as "obligatory" undoubtedly constitute *one* of the various possible determinants of the actual conduct of the "exchange partners." But they only constitute one possible determinant. From the perspective of the observer of the exchange, their actual presence in a concrete case is only an hypothesis.

It should not be forgotten that the presence of these "normative" maxims in a given case also has the status of an hypothesis from the standpoint of each exchange partner in his relation to the other. The following case is, of course, quite familiar. Either or both of the exchange partners knows that the normative "meaning" of the exchange is an ideally "valid" or "prescriptive" norm, a norm which should, in general, be regarded as obligatory. Yet he does *not* treat this normative "meaning" of the exchange as his own "normative maxim." However he speculates on the likelihood that the *other* exchange partner will treat the normative "meaning" of the exchange as his own "normative maxim." In this case, therefore, the maxim employed is pure "prudence" or "utility." Consider the claim that in this case the exchange *is* empirically "regulated" by an ideal norm. In other words, the exchange partners *have* regulated their relations in this fashion. It is obvious that this claim has no empirical import at all. Nevertheless, we occasionally express ourselves in this fashion. This is a consequence of the same ambiguity in the expression "rule-governed" which we noted in the case of the man with the artificially "regulated" digestion. It is harmless as long as we keep in mind exactly *what* the expression is supposed to mean in each concrete case of its use. On the other hand, suppose that the "rule" to which (given the dogmatic "meaning" of their behavior) the exchange partners should have subordinated their conduct is described as the "form" of their "social relation," and therefore as a "form" of the *event*. It is obvious that this would be utterly absurd. The "rule" itself as a product of dogmatic inference only "exists" as a "norm" that has an ideal, putative "validity" *for* action. But it is never a "form" of empirical "existence."

It is obvious that anyone who undertakes to discuss the empirical *existence* of "social life" cannot legitimately base his discussion upon the foundation of axiological dogmatics. Within the domain of "existence," a "rule" can be identified in our example only in the following sense: as an empirical "maxim" that is both causally effective and causally explicable. Given the import of the last of the three concepts of "nature" analyzed on pages 96-97, this point could be expressed in the following way. From the standpoint of logic, the "meaning" of an observable process also falls within the domain of "nature" whenever its *empirical* existence is the object of the investigation. In this case, the object of the investigation is not the "meaning" which is *dogmatically* "ascribed" to the observable process. On the contrary, it is one of the following: either the "meaning" which the "actors" really associate with the process; or the identifiable "indices" of the "meaning" which the "actors" apparently associate with the process. It is obvious that precisely the same point holds for the special case of the *"rule of law."*

Analysis of the Concept of a Rule: The Concept of a "Rule of a Game"

Before we enter the domain of "law" in the usual sense of the word, suppose we clarify certain aspects of our general problem which have not yet been resolved. For this purpose, we shall employ another illustration. From time to time, Stammler himself refers to the analogy of "rules of a game." For our purposes, we shall have to work out this analogy much more thoroughly. To this end, suppose we consider the game of skat as if it were one of those basic elements of culture which "history" generates and which falls within the domain of "social science."

The three skat players "subject their conduct" to the rules of skat. What does this mean? It means that they have adopted the following "normative" maxims. (1) There are certain criteria which *should* establish whether someone has played "correctly"—that is, "in accordance with the norms." (2) And these criteria *should* establish who qualifies as the "winner." From a logical point of view, these propositions can be the object of very different kinds of investigation. The "norm" itself—the rules of the game—could be the object of a purely conceptual discussion. This discussion might have the purpose of practical evaluation. Consider, for example, the "skat congresses" which were formerly held. Suppose that one such congress took up this question. In view of the ("eudaemonistic") "values" which the game of skat serves, would it not be fitting to introduce certain new rules which would govern all future games? This is a question concerning the *politics* of skat. On the other hand, the discussion might have a dogmatic purpose. For example, "must" a certain kind of incentive "consistently" produce a certain ordered sequence of games as its consequence? This is a question in the general theory of the law of skat, posed from the standpoint of "natural law." The following question falls within the domain of the *jurisprudence* of skat in the proper sense. Does a game qualify as "lost" if a player "plays the wrong card"? All questions which concern the issue of whether a player has played "correctly" (that is, according to the norm) or "incorrectly" in a concrete case fall within this domain.

The following, however, is a purely *empirical* question. More precisely, it is an "historical" problem. In a certain instance, why did a player play "incorrectly"? Did he do so wittingly, unwittingly, and so on? The following is a "question of value." However it can be answered in a purely empirical fashion. In a given case, did a player do "well"? In other words, did he play *effectively*? Such an issue can be resolved according to "empirical generalizations"; for example, these generalizations indicate whether a certain play will, in general, increase or decrease the chances of "drawing a ten." Therefore the general rules of the practical reason of skat include experiential propositions. Given knowledge of the "possible" combinations of cards and given everyday experience concerning the manner in which one's fellow players will probably react, these rules can acquire varying degrees of rigor. They are "rules of skill" which can be used to "evaluate" the effectiveness of a player's game.

Finally, a player's conduct could be measured against the "ethical norms of skat." In general, his partner will solemnly reprimand the careless player who has allowed the common opponent to win the game. Consider, however, the following maxim, which is thoroughly reprehensible from the standpoint of a "humanitarian" ethic: the use of the third player as a "sacrificial lamb" in the interest of joint exploitation. From the standpoint of the actual ethics of skat, this maxim does not seem to be too objectionable. Corresponding to the different possible purposes of these evaluations, we can distinguish different kinds of maxims which hold within the empirical domain of skat: "ethical" maxims, maxims of "fair play," and "utilitarian" maxims. From a logical standpoint, these maxims are based upon very different principles of evaluation. In consequence, there are corresponding differences in their "normative" status. They vary from the status of an "absolute," at one extreme, to the status of pure "facticity," at the other. However exactly the same point was established in our discussion of the illustration of the exchange.

The following point also holds both for the exchange and for the game of skat. Suppose that we regard skat from a purely empirical-causal point of view. In that case, consider the status of the various referential axes of those maxims which a normative problematic (the politics of skat, the law of skat) treats as "ideally valid." They are analytically reduced to empirical complexes of ideas which determine the actual conduct of the player. These ideas may be in conflict (for example, the player's interests may dictate a violation of the "maxim of fair play"). Or, more often, they conjointly determine his conduct. The skat player lays his ace on the table for the following reason. On the basis of *his* "interpretation" of the "rules of the game," his general "skat experience" and his "ontological" estimation of the probable combinations of cards, he considers this an adequate means for producing that state of affairs which, given the "rules of the game" as he sees them, would qualify him as the "winner." He calculates as follows. In response to his play, someone else will play a ten. Together with further plays which he anticipates, this will produce the ultimate result. In all of this he counts on the fact that the other players will also follow the "rules of the game" as he sees them. He counts on this fact because he thinks he can depend upon the causal efficacy of their subjective "maxims of fair play." In general, he knows them as men who are disposed to act in accordance with "ethical maxims." On the other hand, he also includes in his deliberations the estimation of a certain probability which, given his knowledge of their qualifications as skat players, amounts to this: from a teleological point of view, they will act more or less "prudently" and in accordance with their own interests. In other words, in concrete cases they also have the capacity to act on "utilitarian maxims." In consequence, the logic of his deliberations, which are decisive for his conduct, may be articulated in propositions of the following form. Suppose that I do x. The other players will not intentionally violate the rule a. In addition, they will play prudently, looking to their own interests. Further, the combination of cards z seems likely. Therefore the probable consequence will be y.

There is no doubt that the "rules of the game" can be described as a *"presupposition"* for a specific play or a given game. However one ought to be clear about what this implies for the empirical inquiry that concerns us here. First of all, the "rules of the game" are a *causal* "factor." This obviously does not hold for the "rules of the game" conceived as an "ideal" norm of the "law of skat." However the idea which the players have at any given time concerning the content and the binding force of these rules is one of the determinants of their actual conduct. Normally each *player* "presupposes" that the other players will treat the "rules of the game" as "maxims" of their conduct. Normally this assumption is in fact made. In consequence, its empirical realization is more *or less* assured. In general, this assumption is a *substantive* "presupposition" of the fact that each of the players really resolves—or, if he is a cheat, seems to resolve— to follow the corresponding maxims. Consider, therefore, a causal explanation of the way a given game of skat was played. It is obvious that the causal regress would have to include the speculation on the part of each player that the other players will in fact follow the usual "rules." It follows that this explanation would also have to take into account the knowledge of these "rules" which they have "acquired." In general, this speculation is invariably an effective determinant of the player's conduct. It has the same status as all the other causal "presuppositions" of his conduct. *In this respect*, there is no difference of any sort between this "presupposition" and those "conditions" on which human life and intentional action depend.

Suppose, however, that the rules of skat are described as the "presupposition" of empirical *knowledge* of skat. It is obvious that the logical import of this claim is essentially different from the logical import of the claim that the rules constitute a "presupposition" for the playing of a given game. The former claim has the following import. In contrast to the other "general," substantive "presuppositions" of the game, we see the rules as the definitive *criterion* of "skat." This claim may be formulated somewhat more carefully as follows. Consider those processes which qualify as *relevant* from the standpoint of a *norm* that is conventionally called "the rules of skat." We see these processes as a complex of performances that constitute a "game of skat." Consider, therefore, the fortuitous "milieu" of a given game of skat: cigar smoke, beer drinking, beating on the table, and deliberations of every conceivable sort which constitute the manifold within which an authentic German skat game is usually played. The conceptual content of this "norm" is decisive for the identification of the elements of this manifold that are "essential to the concept" of skat. Therefore we "classify" a complex of processes as "skat" when the following condition is satisfied: from the standpoint of the application of the norm, these processes qualify as relevant. The causal explanation of these processes is the purpose of an "historical" analysis of the actual playing of a concrete game of skat. These processes constitute the empirical collectivity of a "skat game." They constitute the empirical concept of "skat." In sum: It is relevance from the standpoint of the "norm" which defines the *object* of the investigation. Consider this sense in which the rules of skat are a "presupposition" of empirical knowledge of skat. It is clear that this sense in which the rules of the game constitute a "presupposition" must be strictly *distinguished* from the following sense: knowledge of the rules and their inclusion in the calculations of the players are a "presupposition" of the *playing* of an actual "game of skat." The following point is also clear. Consider the use of this normative concept for the classification and identification of the object, the game of skat. This does not alter the logical properties of the empirical-causal investigation of the object as defined by the use of the normative concept.

The important function of such a normative concept is restricted to the following. Consider the causal explanation of the facts and processes on which an "historical *interest*" would eventually focus. It is by reference to the content of the norm that we identify these facts and processes. In other words, facts and processes that are defined in this way and distinguished from the manifold of the empirically given constitute the point of departure for a causal investigation. Suppose, however, that a causal investigation of a concrete game of skat is undertaken from this beginning point. The inquiry immediately transcends the domain of events which qualify as "relevant" from the standpoint of the norm. In order to provide an "explanation" of the playing of a game of skat, it would be necessary to ascertain, for example, the following: the abilities and education of each player, his "alertness" and its influence upon his capacity for concentration at a given moment, the amount of beer each player has drunk and its influence upon the consistency with which he follows "utilitarian" maxims, and so on. Therefore it is only the *beginning* point of the investigation which is determined by "relevance" from the standpoint of the "norm."

This is an example of a so-called "teleological" conceptual construct. Conceptual constructs of this sort are not limited to the domain of "social" life. They are not even restricted to the domain of "human" life. From the manifold of events and processes, biology "selects" those which are "essential" in a certain "sense": they are "essential" to the "preservation of life." In discussing a work of art, we "select" those aspects of the manifold of phenomena which are "aesthetically essential." This does *not* mean that these aspects have aesthetic "value." On the contrary, it only means that they are "relevant to aesthetic judgments." This holds even if our intention is not to offer an aesthetic "evaluation" of the work of art. It remains true even if our purpose is to establish purely empirical knowledge: for example, an historical-causal "explanation" of the concrete distinctiveness of the work of art or the use of the work of art as an illustration which elucidates certain general causal claims about the conditions for the development of art. The selection or identification of the object of empirical explanation is "determined" by its relation to "values": aesthetic "values," biological "values," or, in our example, the "values" of the law of skat. In these cases, the object does not "exist" as an aesthetic norm, a vitalistic "purpose" of a god or a world spirit, or a doctrine of the law of skat. Just to the contrary. In the case of a work of art, the painting as an object of investigation is made up of brush strokes which are determined by the causally explicable (explicable by reference to "milieu," "talent," "personal fate," concrete "stimuli," etc.) mental states of the artist. In the case of the "organism," the object of investigation is constituted by certain physically observable processes. In the case of the game of skat it is constituted by the ideas and the observable conduct of the players, both of which are determined by empirical "maxims."

A further sense in which the "rules of skat" can be described as a "presupposition" for empirical *knowledge* of skat turns on the following empirical fact. Normally, knowledge and observation of the "rules of skat" are among the empirical "maxims" of skat players. Therefore these "maxims" exercise a causal influence upon their conduct. Obviously it is only *our* knowledge of the "law of skat" which makes it possible for us to establish what sort of influence this is—and, in consequence, to identify the empirical causes of the player's conduct. We employ our knowledge of the ideal "norm" as a "heuristic technique." The historian of art, in quite the same way, employs *his own* (normative) aesthetic "judgment" as an heuristic technique. He employs it as a—de facto—indispensable method for identifying the actual "intentions" of the artist, "intentions" which are germane to a causal explanation of the peculiarities of his work. The same relationship is at stake when we use *general* propositions concerning the "likelihood" that a certain series of plays will be the consequence of a given distribution of cards. In this case we would employ the following "presupposition." (1) The ideal rules of the game (the "laws of skat") are in fact observed. (2) Play is strictly rational or teleologically "utilitarian." In other words, play follows the rules employed in the "skat exercises" (or, in the case of chess, the "chess exercises") that the newspapers publish.[15] In general, experience indicates that players attempt and actually attain a certain "approximation" to this "idealtype." This presupposition would be employed in order to establish the "probability"—which may vary from the significant to the insignificant—that games with this distribution of cards will be played in a way that corresponds to this type.

The "rules of skat," therefore, can have three functions as "presuppositions" of an *empirical* inquiry. From a logical point of view, these three functions are completely different. The rules of the game can be employed for taxonomic and conceptual-constitutive purposes in order to *define* the object of the investigation. They can be employed *heuristically* in order to establish causal *knowledge* of this object. And, finally, they can function as causal *determinants* of the object of knowledge itself. And before we began this discussion of "presuppositions," we established that there are fundamentally different senses in which the rule itself can constitute an object of knowledge. From the standpoint of the politics and jurisprudence of skat, a rule constitutes an "ideal" norm. From an empirical point of view, it is both an actual cause and an effect. The following preliminary conclusion may be drawn from this discussion. It is absolutely necessary to establish as precisely as possible the *sense* in which the "meaning" of a "rule" constitutes a "presupposition" of any sort of knowledge. And most important: Unless every source of ambiguity in these expressions is carefully resolved, the constant danger of hopeless confusion between the empirical and the normative will inevitably reach its upper limit.

Analysis of the Concept of a Rule: The Concept of a Rule of Law

At this point let us move from the domain of the "conventional" norms of skat and the quasi-"jurisprudence" of the "law of skat" to "genuine" *law* (at this point we shall not consider the question of the definitive difference between a legal and a conventional rule). Recall our earlier illustration of the "exchange." Let us suppose that this exchange transpires within the domain of the validity of a positive system of law, a system of law which "governs" the exchange. Given these assumptions, it *appears* that, in addition to the complications discussed above, a further problem arises. In the formation of the *empirical* concept of "skat," the *norm* of skat is a conceptually definitive "presupposition" in the following sense: it determines the extension of the object. It is conduct *relevant* to the *law* of skat which determines the points of departure for an empirical-historical analysis of skat. Suppose, however, that a legal construct is investigated. And suppose that this investigation is not concerned with legal dogmatics, or even with historical problems that are purely *legal*. On the contrary, suppose that this investigation falls within the domain of "cultural history" or the "theory of culture"—we shall use these expressions quite generally at this point. The problem which *apparently* arises is the following: The relationship between a rule of law and the actual course of human "cultural life" is not the same as the relationship between a rule of skat and the playing of an actual game of skat.[16]

This point may be expressed in the following preliminary and extremely equivocal fashion. Consider the causal development of certain aspects of reality that are regulated by the ideal norms of a law. Suppose we attempt to explain this causal development in relation to "cultural values" that are important from an "historical" point of view. Or suppose we attempt to establish (from the perspective of a theory of culture) general propositions concerning the causal conditions for the existence of these aspects of reality or general propositions concerning their causal consequences. The foregoing discussions were concerned with an empirical-historical inquiry into a concrete "game of skat." The constitution of the object (the historical "entity") was determined by the relevance of the facts from the standpoint of the "norms of skat." In an inquiry that is not merely concerned with law, but rather with "cultural" history, legal norms simply do not have this status. In classifying facts as economic, political, and so on, we also employ extralegal criteria. Facts of cultural life that are of no legal relevance at all are also of historical "interest" to us. In any given case, therefore, the following question remains open. Consider the properties of a given collection of facts which are *relevant* from the standpoint of an ideally valid law and the legal concepts formed in accordance with it. To what extent are these properties also *relevant* to concept formation in history or "cultural theory"?[17] In principle, therefore, the legal norm loses its status as the "presupposition" for the formation of the collective concept.

But it does *not* follow that these two kinds of conceptual schemes are logically independent. The relationship between them is not that simple. As we shall see, this is because legal *terms* are quite regularly employed in conceptual schemes that are of relevance to perspectives which are radically different from the perspective of law; for example, the perspective of economics. Moreover it does not follow this this usage should simply be repudiated as a terminological mistake. In the first place, a legal concept may prove to be very useful *empirically*. Quite often it has functioned and it could function as an "archetype" of the corresponding economic concept. Further, it is obvious that the "empirically existing legal order"—a concept we shall discuss very shortly—is in general of considerable significance to economically relevant facts (for the present, we shall only make this claim in a very general fashion). But—and we shall also discuss this point in the ensuing—these two kinds of conceptual schemes are certainly not equivalent. Consider, for example, the concept of "exchange." In this case, the economic problematic is extended to include facts of the most heterogeneous legal character. That is because these facts have properties that are of relevance to the problematic of economics. In addition, as we shall see, an economic problematic is quite often concerned with the distinctive features of properties that have absolutely no legal relevance. In the ensuing we shall often have occasion to return to the problems posed by the relationship between these two kinds of conceptual schemes. For the present, we shall only take up the following preliminary points. First, we shall show that the various logically possible problematics identified in our analysis of the game of skat also reappear in the analysis of "legal rules." Further, we shall indicate the limits of this analogy in a purely provisional fashion. At this point, we shall not attempt to provide a correct and conclusive formulation of its logical content.[18] We shall consider these questions in more detail later, after we have learned from *Stammler's* arguments how *not* to deal with these problems.

**Analysis of the Concept of a Rule:
Legal and Empirical Concepts**

Different kinds of questions can be raised about a given "paragraph" of the code of civil law. Consider first *political* questions. We can discuss the normative "justification" of the paragraph from the standpoint of ethical principles. Or we can consider it from the perspective of "cultural ideals" or political postulates—postulates of "power politics" or postulates of "welfare politics"—and discuss its advantages or disadvantages from the standpoint of the realization of these ideals. Or we can consider it from the perspective of "class" or personal interests and discuss the respects in which it "serves" or "prejudices" these interests. We have already considered this sort of analysis of the "rule"—an analysis that is clearly axiological—in our discussion of "skat." This sort of analysis poses no new problems of logical principle. For the present, therefore, we shall say nothing further about it. There are two further questions that can be raised about the paragraph. We can ask: What is its *conceptual "import"*? And we can ask: What does it *in fact "achieve"* or *"produce"*? Are the answers to these two questions a presupposition for a fruitful discussion of the problem of the ethical, political, or other value of the paragraph? This is an entirely different question. Put another way, it is quite obvious that the question of the value of the paragraph is completely independent of this last pair of issues. Therefore a strict distinction must be made between these issues and the question of value.

Let us examine the essential logical properties of these two questions. In both cases, the grammatical subject of the question is "it": that is to say, the specific "paragraph" in the code of civil law. However the objects to which the word "it" refers in these two questions are utterly different. In the first case, "it" refers to the "paragraph" itself: a set of conceptual relations expressed in words. It is always possible to conceive this conceptual construct as a purely ideal object of conceptual analysis, refined and purified by the legal scholar. In the second case, however, "it"—the "paragraph"—refers to the following empirical fact. Suppose that someone opens one of those volumes called the "Code of Civil Law" and turns to a passage where a certain expression is used regularly. And suppose that—by employing the basic rules of "interpretation" in which he has in fact been educated—he understands this expression more or less clearly and precisely. Given this understanding, certain ideas about the actual consequences which might follow a certain kind of observable behavior occur to him. In general, this state of affairs has the following empirical consequence—although, in fact, this consequence is certainly not invariable. Certain psychological and physical "instruments of coercion" are at the disposal of a certain person. This person knows how to employ a certain technique for persuading other persons, usually called "judges," that this particular kind of "observable behavior" occurred or very probably occurred in a given case. This state of affairs also has a further consequence. Anyone can "count on" the fact that the behavior of other persons in their relationship to him will be of a certain sort—even if he does not call upon the assistance of those persons called "judges." This fact has a very high degree of probability. In other words, there is a certain *probability* that we can count on the unmolested use of a certain object. Therefore we can—and we do—structure our affairs on the basis of this probability. In this last case—in which the paragraph concerns an empirical fact—the empirical "validity" of the "paragraph" is constituted by complex causal relationships which hold within the domain of empirical-historical reality: real conduct of men in relation to one another and to extra-human "nature," conduct which is a consequence of the fact that a certain piece of paper is covered with certain "letters."[19]

But consider the "validity" of a legal maxim in the first sense mentioned above, the "ideal" sense. From the standpoint of the scholarly conscience of the person who *wants* to establish "juristic truth," it is constituted by a rigorous logical relationship between *concepts*. In other words, it is constituted by the "*axiological* validity" which a certain logic has for the legal mind. On the other hand, consider the following *fact. In general*, actual persons who *want* to establish "juristic truth" are *disposed* to infer the "axiological validity" of a certain "legal maxim" from certain verbal relationships. This fact is. obviously not without empirical consequences. On the contrary, it is of the greatest conceivable empirical-historical significance. Simply consider the fact that a "jurisprudence" exists. And consider the "intellectual habits" which are actually governed by this "jurisprudence," habits which develop in an empirical-historical fashion. This fact is of tremendous practical-empirical significance for the actual organization of human affairs. The reason for this is as follows. Within empirical reality there are "judges" and other "officials" who are in a position to influence human behavior by employing certain physical and psychological instruments of coercion. They have been educated in such a way that they *want* to establish "juristic truth." And—actually, with very different degrees of consistency—they conform to these "maxims." Our "social life" is empirically "regulated." In the present context, this means that it transpires within the limits of "regularities" in the following sense: each day, the butcher, the baker, and the newspaper boy adapt themselves to this "empirical" regularity. This "empirical" regularity is obviously one of the most fundamental consequences of the empirical existence of a "legal order."

To say that a "legal order" in fact exists is to say that it exists as a "maxim," an idea of something *obligatory*. This "maxim" is a causal determinant of human conduct. The following point, however, is obvious: Not only these empirical regularities, but also the empirical "existence" of "law," are completely different from the legal idea of the *"axiological* validity" of law. "Empirical" validity can be ascribed to both "juristic truth" and "juristic error" in exactly the same degree. Consider the question: *What* is "juristic truth"? That is to say, in view of certain "objective" principles of jurisprudence as a scholarly discipline, what logically *should* be "valid," or what should *have been* "valid"? The logical import of this question is entirely different from the import of the following question: In a concrete case or in a plurality of cases, what in fact *followed* as the empirical, causal "consequence" of the "validity" of a certain "paragraph"? In the first case, the "rule of law" is an ideal, conceptually deducible *norm*. In the second case, it is an empirically *ascertainable maxim* of the concrete conduct of human beings, a *maxim* they may follow more or less frequently and consistently. In the first case, a "legal order" is constituted by a system of ideas and concepts which the scholar in jurisprudence uses as a standard of value. He employs this system in order to make juristic evaluations of the actual conduct of certain men—"judges," "attorneys," "delinquents," "citizens," and so on. Such an evaluation determines whether their conduct is admissible or inadmissible from the standpoint of the ideal norm. In the second case, a "legal order" may be analyzed as a complex of maxims in the minds of certain men who really exist. These maxims have a causal influence upon their actual conduct. In consequence, they indirectly influence the conduct of others.

Thus far, the matter is relatively simple. It becomes more complicated when we consider the relationship between the *legal* concept of the "United States" and the empirical-historical "structure" of the same name. From a logical point of view, they are two different things. This is because the following question invariably arises. To what extent are the facts which acquire *relevance* from the standpoint of the rule of law also relevant for the empirical-historical, political, and socioscientific inquiry? We should not be misled by the fact that both the legal entity and the historical entity have the same *name*. Consider the following six propositions. "The United States, unlike its member states, is empowered to conclude commerical treaties." "Accordingly, the United States has concluded a commercial treaty of a certain content a with Mexico." "However the commercial interests of the United States require a treaty of content b." "This is because the United States exports quantity d of product c to Mexico." "Therefore the balance of payments of the United

States will have the value x." "This must have the influence y on the value of the United States dollar." In each of these six propositions, the expression "United States" is used in a different sense.[20] At this point, therefore, the analogy with the "skat" example breaks down.

The empirical concept of a concrete "game of skat" is logically equivalent to those processes which are relevant from the standpoint of the *law* of skat. Unlike the concept of the "United States," we have no reason to use the concept "skat" in different ways.[21] This is obviously related to the disposition mentioned above: the inclination to employ legal *terminology* (for example, the concept of "exchange") in other areas. Let us make another attempt to clarify more precisely—at least in its broadest outlines—the logical consequences of this inclination. First a few remarks by way of recapitulation. As we have already established, it is absurd to claim that the following relationship obtains between the rule of law and "social life." Law can be conceived as the—or as a—"form" of "social life." It is to be distinguished from the "substance" or "matter" of "social life." It would also be absurd to undertake to deduce the "logical" consequences of this view. The rule of law, conceived as an "idea," is neither an empirical regularity nor a "rule-governed process." On the contrary, it is a norm which can be *conceived* as having "axiological validity." Therefore it is quite obviously not a form of *being* or *existence*, but rather a standard of value by reference to which empirical existence can be evaluated *if* we are interested in "juristic truth." *Empirically* conceived, however, the rule of law is not really a "form" of social life— regardless of how the concept of social life might be conceptually defined. It is an objective component of empirical reality. It is a *maxim*, a causal determinant of the empirically observable behavior of—in any given case—an indefinitely large plurality of men. In any given case it is followed more or less "strictly" and more or less consciously and consistently.

Consider the following facts. On the basis of their experience, judges follow the "maxim" of "deciding conflicts of interest" by reference to a certain rule of law. Other people—bailiffs, police, and so on—are guided by the "maxim" that they should "carry out" this decision. Further, most people in general think "legally." In other words, they normally internalize rules of law as maxims of their own conduct. These are all features—uncommonly important features—of the empirical reality of life. They are especially important properties of "social life." Let us define the empirical "legal order" as follows. It is the "empirical *existence*" of law conceived as "knowledge" possessed by concrete men, "knowledge" which is constitutive for the formation of maxims. This knowledge—in other words, this "empirical legal order"—is one of the determinants of the conduct of the human agent. To some extent it is an "obstacle." Insofar as he acts purposefully, the human agent attempts to master it, either by violating it as prudently as possible or by "adapting" himself to it. To some extent it is a "means" that he tries to use in pursuing his own "aims." In this respect, this knowledge has the same status as his knowledge of any other empirical proposition. Suppose he attempts to change the empirical legal order in accordance with his "interests"—in the long run, by influencing other people. From a logical point of view he does this in exactly the same way that he attempts to change some natural phenomenon by the technological mastery of the forces of nature.

Let us employ an example that Stammler also uses. Suppose that a man can no longer endure the fumes of a chimney in the neighborhood. In that event, he consults his own experiential knowledge or the knowledge of some other person (an "attorney," for example) on the following question. Suppose that certain pieces of paper are served at a certain place (the "court"). And suppose that certain people called "judges" follow certain procedures. And suppose that there is a piece of paper (called a "decision") which—if it is signed by the "judges"—is "sufficient" to produce the following result: certain persons are psychologically or—if necessary—physically coerced so that they no longer fire this particular furnace. Will these people called "judges" sign this piece of paper called a "judgment"? Suppose that our man tries to determine whether there is some probability that this result can be expected. Then it is obvious that either he or his "attorney" will be most interested in the answer to the following question. Given the "conceptual" *import* of the rule of law, how "should" the judges decide the case? Of course this "dogmatic" inquiry into the content of the law will not win his case. For his empirical purposes, even the most "objective" result of such an inquiry is only *one* of the indices germane to the calculation of the probability of the actual empirical result. Suppose that his attorney undertakes a conscientious investigation of the legal meaning of the "norm" and concludes that the case should be decided in favor of his client. Nevertheless, as the client very well knows, there may be innumerable reasons why he may "lose the game" in court. This colloquial way of expressing the matter is appropriate and very significant.

As a matter of fact, the *judicial process* is perfectly analogous to the "game of skat," and presumably no further discussion is necessary in order to establish this. In the judicial process, the empirical legal order is a "presupposition" of the empirical process: the "maxims" employed by the judges who decide the case and the "means" employed by the parties to the dispute. Knowledge of the conceptual "import" of the law—in other words, knowledge of its meaning as established by dogmatics or jurisprudence—is also an essential heuristic technique for the empirical-causal "explanation" of the actual proceedings of a concrete judicial process. The legal order, therefore, has the same status occupied by the rules of skat in an "historical" analysis of a skat game. Moreover the legal order is also constitutive for the definition of the "historical entity." Suppose we attempt to provide a causal explanation of a concrete judicial process as a *judicial process*. In such an "explanation," it is the legally *relevant* aspects of the process which are of interest. Therefore the analogy between the legal order and the rules of skat is complete. The empirical concept of the concrete "case of law"—exactly like the empirical concept of a concrete game of *skat*—is exhaustively defined by reference to those aspects of reality which are relevant from the standpoint of the "rule of law"—or, in the case of skat, those aspects of reality which are relevant from the standpoint of the "rules of skat."

But suppose that we are not concerned with a "history" of a concrete "case of *law*." In other words, we are not interested in an explanation of the juridical result. Suppose that we are interested in the "history" of an object on which the legal order has a preponderant influence; for example, "labor relations" in a specific industry, like the textile industry in Saxony. In this case, the logical relationships under discussion here are considerably altered. Are the matters that "interest" us now necessarily limited to those aspects of reality which are of relevance to some "rule of *law*"? Not at all. It is obviously quite incontestable that, regardless of our "problematic," law is of enormous causal significance for "labor relations." It is one of the general *objective* "conditions" which the investigation of "labor relations" must take into account. Recall the relationship which we noted between the "rules of skat" and the concrete game of skat and the relationship between the legal rule and the judicial process. That relationship no longer obtains in this case. This is because the facts which are "relevant" from the standpoint of law are *no* longer *necessarily* the components of the "historical entity." In other words, they are not *necessarily* the facts which have peculiarities that "interest" us, the facts for which we "require" a causal explanation. Of course the specific properties of the concrete "legal order" which exists at any given time and place may be one of the most decisive causal "conditions" for the explanation of these facts. Moreover the *mere existence* of a "legal order" is just as much a general, indispensable (*substantive*) "presupposition" of these facts as the presence of wool, cotton, or flax and their value for the satisfaction of certain human needs.

Although we shall not do this here, we might try to construct a series of kinds of possible objects of investigation. This series would satisfy the following condition. In each successive object of investigation included in the series, the general causal significance of the concrete *definitive properties* of the "empirical legal order" is gradually and continuously diminished. The definitive properties of other conditions would gradually acquire an increasing causal significance. From such a series we could try to draw some general causal conclusions about the extent to which empirically existing legal orders are of causal importance for cultural facts. At this juncture, our only concern is to establish the following general point. In principle, the causal importance of empirically existing legal orders for cultural facts is variable. These variations are a function of the properties of the object of investigation. Consider, for example, the distinctive aesthetic qualities of the Sistine Chapel Madonna. They "presuppose" an empirical "legal order" with characteristics that are quite specific. This "legal order" would have to appear as an "explanans" in any exhaustive causal explanation of the Sistine Chapel Madonna. Moreover, independent of the existence of some "legal order" as a general "causal condition," the empirical probability of the creation of this work of art would be vanishing small. But what of the facts that constitute the "historical entity": "the Sistine Chapel Madonna"? They are of no *legal* relevance at all.

Of course it is understandable that the professional jurist is biased in favor of a general conception of cultural man as a potential plaintiff. In exactly the same sense, the shoemaker sees him as a prospective customer, and the skat player sees him as a potential "third party." But it is obvious that they would be quite mistaken if they claimed that cultural man is a possible object of the sociocultural sciences only to the extent that he is a potential customer or card player. Consider a jurist who is convinced that human relationships are possible components of an "historical entity" only to the extent that they are *relevant* to a possible judicial process. Suppose this belief leads him to the conclusion that man is a possible object of the sociocultural sciences only insofar as he is a *"potential player in the judicial* process." This is obviously a mistake too. Actual criteria for explanation can be concerned with aspects of reality—especially the relationships of human conduct and relationships between human conduct and the extra-human natural world—which are of no "legal" relevance at all. Criteria of this sort are employed regularly in the praxis of the sociocultural sciences. On the other hand—and the earlier remarks on this point should be added here by way of supplementation—important branches of the empirical sociocultural sciences, especially political and economic disciplines, employ legal concepts for terminological purposes. We have already stressed this point. The following consideration, however, is more important. They also employ these concepts for the purpose of what might be called a *preliminary* analysis of their own subject matter.

Consider the use of legal concepts for a provisional classification of the heterogeneous manifold of relationships in which we are actually enmeshed. This use of legal concepts is chiefly due to the advanced state of the development of legal thought. Therefore it is always necessary to keep the following point clearly in mind. Suppose that a political or economic inquiry undertakes to conceive its subject matter in terms of the "problematic" of politics or economics. In that case, legal concepts acquire a facticity that necessarily changes their meaning. Whenever this happens, the inquiry is no longer at the level on which a preliminary analysis is undertaken by employing legal concepts. Nothing would obscure recognition of this point more than the following error. Because of these important functions of the legal conceptual framework, the legal rule is elevated to the status of a "formal principle" of knowledge of human social life. It is very easy to fall into this error for the following reason. The *actual* importance of the empirically existing "legal order" is very considerable.

In view of what we have said thus far on this point, consider the following. Suppose that an inquiry is no longer concerned with processes which qualify as "interesting" *solely* because of their *legal* relevance. In that case, it follows that the "legal rule" no longer has the status of a "presupposition"—a regulative principle for the definition of the objects of inquiry. On the other hand, the number of inquiries into human relationships in which "law" is of *causal* significance—in comparison with the causal significance of the rules of skat, for example—is extraordinarily large. The reasons are as follows. Normally the legal rule is in fact endowed with powers of coercion. Moreover the domain within which the validity of the legal rule is acknowledged usually approximates completeness. In general, a given man is not obliged to play skat. Therefore the consequences of the empirical "validity" of the rules of skat need not apply to him. On the other hand, it is de facto impossible for anyone to avoid the constant encounter with facts that are "relevant" from the standpoint of empirically existing legal orders. It begins even before his birth. From an empirical point of view, therefore, he cannot avoid becoming a perpetual "potential player in the game of law." It follows that he is obliged to adapt his behavior to this situation, either on grounds of pure prudence or out of respect for maxims of fair play. In this sense, a purely empirical sense, it is clear that the existence of a "legal order" is certainly included among those universal empirical "presuppositions" of actual conduct *of this sort*, conduct in which men are related to one another and to the extra-human world. This sort of conduct is a necessary condition for the existence of "cultural phenomena." In *this* sense, the "legal order" is only an empirical fact. In this respect, it is comparable to a certain minimum quantity of solar energy. It is simply a *causal* "condition," one of the determinants of this sort of conduct. Suppose that at a certain time and place a certain concrete "fact" falls within the domain of the "legal order." The points which have just been made concerning the status of the empirical "objective legal order" also apply to this fact.

Recall our example of the smoky chimney. It provides an illustration of one such fact: the annoying consequences of the smoke. The "legal order" offers the prospect of a protective remedy to the neighbor who does not want to tolerate these consequences. He has a corresponding "subjective right" to this sort of protection. From the standpoint of an economic problematic, this "subjective right" only represents an *empirical probability*. This probability includes the following components. (1) The "judges" will strictly adhere to the "maxim" that the decision should be made "in accordance with the norm." In other words, the judges are conscientious and cannot be bribed. (2) The judges and the plaintiff—or his attorney—will "interpret" the import of the legal norm in the same way. (3) The actual evidence can be produced which, in the view of the judges, is conclusive for the application of that "norm." (4) The actual enforcement of the judgment will follow, executed in accordance with the requirements of the judges' decision. This probability is "calculable" in the same *logical* sense as the properties of any "technological" process or the likelihood of winning a game of skat. Suppose that the plaintiff wins his case. Then there is no doubt that the "legal rule" has causally influenced the fact that the chimney will no longer smoke—notwithstanding Stammler's claim that this is impossible. But it is obvious that it is not the "legal rule" *conceived* as an ideal "obligation" ("norm") which has this influence. On the contrary, it is the "legal rule" *conceived* as a "maxim" in the minds of the parties concerned: the judges, for example. As such, it is a causal *determinant* of their actual conduct in rendering a "judgment." For the same reason, it is also a causal *determinant* of the conduct of the plaintiff or his legal representative.

The sense in which the "empirical legal order" is a "rule" has the same status. Consider the following verifiable fact, recognized as such by a multitude of persons. The "judge" applies a "maxim" to certain *generally* defined facts in such a way that, in general, conflicts of interest which have the same properties are decided in the same way. In other words, consider the fact that "legal norms" have the properties of generalizations. They are *"rules* of law" and as such they exist as "maxims" in the minds of judges. This circumstance, both directly and indirectly, produces *empirical* regularities in the actual conduct of men in their relations to one another and to commodities. Naturally I am not suggesting that in general the empirical regularities of "cultural life" constitute "projections" of "legal rules." However the fact that the law functions as a "rule" *can* be a "sufficient" condition for these empirical regularities. The law, therefore, is *one* of the various causal determinants of this empirical regularity. As a causal determinant, it occupies a preeminent status. This is clearly a consequence of the fact that real men are normally "reasonable." From an empirical standpoint, this means that they are able to understand "utilitarian maxims" and follow them. They are able to acquire "normative ideas." This is the reason why, at least under certain circumstances, the empirical regularity produced by the legal "regulation" of human conduct *may be* more complete than the empirical, physiological regularity produced by the medical "regulation" of human digestion. Suppose that in a given case an empirically existing "legal rule"–that is, a "maxim" employed by specific persons–is a causal determinant of empirical regularities. Its causal efficacy is subject to extensional and intensional variations from one case to another. Moreover its status as a

causal determinant of empirical regularities is not susceptible
to any general definition.

Consider the following regularities: the empirically "regular" appearance of the bureaucrat in his office; the empirically regular appearance of the butcher in the meat shop; the
empirical regularities in our disposal of the money and the
commodities that we possess; the periodicity of phenomena
called "crises" and "unemployment";[22] the manner in which
"prices" fluctuate with the harvest; the manner in which the
birth rate within a certain population varies with an increase
in "wealth" or intellectual "culture." The sense in which and
the extent to which empirically existing "legal rules" constitute causal determinants in each of these cases are altogether
different. Consider the "effect" of the fact that a new "law"
is "made." A given empirical plurality of people is *disposed*
to *see* the "establishment" of legal rules in a certain way:
both as normal and as binding. A "symbolic" process corresponding to this way of *seeing* takes place. This is the
"effect" of the fact that a new "law" is "made." The "effect" of this fact upon the *actual* behavior of these people
and *others* whom they can influence is in principle susceptible to experiential "calculation." This effect can be calculated *in exactly the same way* as the effect of any "natural
phenomenon." Therefore it is possible to formulate general
empirical propositions about these "effects." They have the
same import as any other proposition of the form: y follows
x. Everyone is familiar with this fact from the everyday
world of politics. Consider *empirical* "rules" which express
the adequate "effect" of the empirical validity of a law.
Compare them with dogmatic "rules" which can be derived
as logical "consequences" of exactly the same law if it is
conceived as an object of "jurisprudence." From a logical
standpoint, these two sorts of "rules" are extreme polar
antitheses. *Both* a dogmatic problematic and an empirical
problematic begin in the same way with the same empirical
"fact": the fact that a legal rule with a certain context is

acknowledged as valid. But then they proceed to raise completely different questions about this "fact." This is why empirical rules and dogmatic rules are polar antitheses. A "dogmatic" inquiry can be called "formal" because its domain is the world of "concepts." The "dogmatic" in this sense is to be distinguished from the "empirical," the domain of causal inquiry in general. If we wish, we may call the empirical causal "conception" of "rules of law"—in contrast to the conception of juristic dogmatics or jurisprudence—"naturalistic." However we ought to be clear about the following point. Given this distinction, "nature" refers to the totality of empirical being in general. Therefore it follows that, from the standpoint of logic, the *"history* of law" is a "naturalistic" discipline too. This is because its object is the *facticity* of the legal norm and not its ideal *meaning*.[2,3]

At this point we shall not analyze the idea of a "conventional rule" and establish its relationship to factual "regularities." Stammler provides an analysis of the concept of a "conventional rule," and we shall discuss it shortly. "Conventional rules" and "legal rules" are alike in the following respect. From a logical point of view, there are fundamental differences between the "rule" as an imperative and the "rule" as an empirical "regularity." From the standpoint of an investigation of *empirical* regularities, the "conventional rule" is also the same as the "legal rule" in this respect: it is one of the *causal* determinants of the object of the investigation. Like the "legal rule," it is neither a "form" of being nor a "formal principle" of knowledge.

In any case, the reader has surely had enough of this fare, a fatiguing account of truths that are utterly self-evident, an account which is even more laborious because of its extremely crude and imprecise language. As I noted, the imprecision of language is due to the fact that the present analysis is only provisional. However the reader should be able to see that the sophisms of Stammler's book are responsible for the unfortunate necessity of introducing these distinctions. This is because all of the sophistical and paradoxical "impressions" that Stammler strives for and actually produces are, in part, consequences of his constant confusion of the following concepts: "rule-like," 'rule-governed,' "legally rule-governed," "rule," "maxim," "norm," "rule of law"—"rule of law" as an object of conceptual analysis in jurisprudence and "rule of law" as an empirical phenomenon, a causal determinant of human action. "Is" and "ought," the "concept" and the "object of the concept" are in a perpetual state of flux. We have already noted this property of Stammler's work. And, as we have seen, Stammler repeatedly confuses the different senses in which the "rule" is a presupposition.

Suppose that Stammler reads this essay. He would probably be inclined to emphasize the following point. Everything or almost everything which has been subjected to extensive criticism in this paper can be found correctly stated and sometimes explicitly emphasized at many different points in his book. In particular, he repeatedly stresses the following point. The "legal order" could obviously become the object of a purely causal inquiry just as well as it could become the object of a "teleological" inquiry. Of course! We shall have to establish the same point. For the present, let us ignore the errors underlying Stammler's discussion of this point, errors which we will consider in the ensuing. Above all, we want to stress the following result of our analysis. In other parts of his book—and even in the most *crucial* passages—Stammler completely forgets these simple truths and their equally trivial consequences. Of course this forgetfulness proves to be very useful in creating the "impressions" which the book produces. Let us suppose that at the outset Stammler had clearly declared that he was exclusively concerned with *axiological* questions. Suppose he had said that he only wanted to point out a "formal principle": a guide for the legislator who deals with the question of lawmaking and the judge who attempts to exercise "judgment." And suppose that Stammler had actually attempted to identify this "formal principle." Regardless of how we might evaluate Stammler's own solution to this particular problem, an enterprise of this sort would certainly create a certain interest. However it is quite obvious that such an inquiry would be absolutely irrelevant to empirical "social science." And, most important, Stammler would have no reason at all to write his extensive and imprecise account of the nature of "social life." At this point, we turn to the criticism of that account. At the same time, we shall provide a further analysis of the dichotomy which thus far has only been sketched in a preliminary fashion: the distinction between empirical and dogmatic conceptual schemes.

Postscript to the Essay on Stammler's "Refutation" of the Materialist Conception of History

"Causality and Teleology" in Stammler's Work

On page 372 of his book, Stammler makes the following claim. "Whenever . . . we are concerned with the *causation* of human conduct, then we find ourselves within the domain of the *natural sciences*." And in relation to this he says (the emphasis is *Stammler's*!) that *the only "causes"* of action are physiological. Then he goes on to articulate this point more precisely: The "causal determinants of action" are said to "lie in the *nervous system*." It is unlikely that this position would be acceptable to a contemporary advocate of any of the various theories concerning the relationship between physical and mental processes. On the one hand, this view is equivalent to "materialism" in the strict sense. At least this is the case if it amounts to the following two claims. First, "action" must be deducible *from* physical processes in order to constitute a possible object of causal explanation *in general*. And second, in principle, the possibility of such a deduc-

145

tion may always in fact be presupposed. On the other hand, this position leaves a back door open for indeterminism. Whatever is not "material"—in other words, whatever is not deducible *from* physical processes—is excluded *in principle* from the domain of causal inquiry.

An ambiguity which has a similar kind of result is found on pages 339-340 of Stammler's book. At this point Stammler claims that first-person conduct can be conceived in two very different ways: "either as a causally determined event in *observable* (note!) nature or as an event *of which I am the cause.*" "In the first case I acquire" (does he really mean here: I *try to discover*?) "established scientific knowledge of specific actions as observable (note!) processes... In the second case a scientific account (what sort of scientific account?) of the causal necessitation of the action in question is not possible. The action is (note!) empirically possible. But it is *not* intrinsically (?) *necessary.*" In the first disjunct of this dichotomy, the obscurity which results from the completely unintentional restriction of the concept of "action" to exclusively "observable" processes is all too obvious. A causal inquiry also investigates the "inner" aspects of events. It considers the idea of the action as "causally" explicable. It also takes into account deliberation over "means" and, finally, deliberation about the "purpose" of the action. From the standpoint of a causal inquiry, all these processes, and not just "external" events, are strictly determined.

In the following passage (Stammler, p. 340, first paragraph), Stammler himself seems to grasp this point. Here he refers to the inquiry into "human action as a natural phenomenon." Then (Stammler, p. 340, second paragraph) he says that "someone who is hungry and thirsty... craves food... He has a *causal compulsion* to eat." This "craving" obviously lies within the domain of the "psychological." In other words, it is not "external" and directly "observable." On the contrary, it can only be "inferred" from "external" observations. And in any case—given Stammler's own terminology—the acquisition and consumption of food is an "action." It can be based upon very different degrees of reflection about "means" and "ends." There is a continuous spectrum of cases varying from the most unreflective "swilling" to the most sophistricated selection of a dinner from the menu of a first-class restaurant. No sharp, definitive distinctions can be made within this spectrum of cases. However it is obvious that every conceivable nuance—from the thoroughly "impulsive" to the completely "reflective" action—is an object of *causal* inquiry in precisely the same sense. Such an inquiry invariably presupposes the complete determination of its subject matter. On pages 342–343, Stammler considers Ihering's distinction between "mechanical" and "psychological" causality. Ihering defines "psychological" causality by reference to *teleological* ideas. Stammler rejects this distinction because there is no unambiguous and definitive substantive difference between the two kinds of causality. But in his own illustrations only two pages before these remarks, Stammler himself carefully distinguishes "rational" and "impulsive" conduct.[24] Why? This is not a result of carelessness on Stammler's part. Just to the contrary. At this point, Stammler reverses himself and accepts Ihering's dichotomy unreservedly.

On page 340 in the third paragraph, we find the following claims. (1) The "idea" (note!) of unsatisfied human hunger lies within the domain of causal knowledge of nature *if* "the process of eating qualifies as a causally necessary consequence of *instinctive drives*" (note!). Example: "The infant nursing at its mother's breast." (2) On the other hand, "Imagine the following event (note!) . . . . We prepare and finish off (!) a fine banquet. This *is certainly not* an inevitable necessity" (note!). "Just to the contrary, it *can only be brought about* by the actor himself." Here again the "style of imprecision" noted in our earlier discussion is unmistakable. Proposition (1) creates the impression that *only* "instinctual" processes are possible objects of a *causal* analysis. However this view is not made explicit. Consider proposition (2), which places the "banquet" within the "Kingdom of freedom." It scrupulously avoids an answer to the question: *Whose* "idea" or "knowledge," and so on is at stake here? Is it the "idea" of the actor himself, who may have the "idea" on one occasion but not on another? Or is it *"our"* "idea," the "idea" of the investigator who regards the actor as an *object* from the standpoint of various *problematics*? It seems that in proposition (1), which concerns the "idea of unsatisfied hunger," it is the idea of the inquirer that Stammler has in mind. In the case of the "fine banquet," however, Stammler seems to be thinking of the idea of the person who is eager to—in Stammler's words—"finish it off." Otherwise the form of words he employs in the conclusion—"it can only *be* brought about by the actor himself"—makes no sense. In other words, we encounter one more example of the conflation of the subject and object of knowledge which Stammler favors so often. By this means he is able to evade clarity of expression completely.

This sort of confusion persists throughout the entire chapter called "Causality and Teleology." The account contained on pages 374–375 would have been quite sufficient as a presentation of all the *valid points* that Stammler has to make in this section of Book Four. Consider a scientific, moral, or aesthetic insight. Consider also the question: Is this insight *sound*, and if so, on what "grounds" is its soundness based? A rigorous distinction must be made between this question and the issue: What "causes" are *responsible for the origin* of this insight? As Stammler himself notes quite correctly at this point, these two questions articulate two completely *different* problematics. If this is the case, then what is the meaning of Stammler's remark at the middle of page 375, where he says that the question concerning the "systematic meaning"—in other words, the *validity*—of an insight is both "the *principal substantive* question and also the decisive issue"? But *for whom*? Moreover it seems that in the first paragraph on page 374, Stammler also concedes the legitimacy of a strictly empirical investigation of the genesis of all the "ideational" contents of life. At this point, Stammler considers the possibility of "complete" knowledge of the conditions for the existence of an "idea." He claims that "it is *possible* to deduce the *empirical* (the emphasis is Stammler's!) consequences of these given conditions—the fact that something does or does not occur—just as rigorously as it is possible to deduce the occurrence of any other natural phenomenon." But even the manner in which Stammler expresses himself here is curiously tortured. In spite of "complete" knowledge, the deduction only seems to be "possible." Instead of making the straightforward claim that the empirical existence of the "idea" is unequivocally determined, he introduces the concept of an "empirical effect" and explicates it in an ambiguous fashion. The explication is ambiguous for the following reasons. The expression "empirical effect" calls to mind Stammler's restriction of causal inquiry to "external" or "observable" (physiological) processes. We cited this limitation in the foregoing. Moreover many remarks, both in the chapter "Causality and Teleology" and in the chapter that immediately follows it, have the following force. Consider an admission which Stammler makes repeatedly: an empirical inquiry is just as legitimate within the domain of "ideas" as it is within any other domain of reality. This admission is also *repeatedly* subjected to similar qualifications. In some cases it is completely *retracted*. Finally, Stammler's remarks concerning the significance and the limits of empirical-causal knowledge of human action are completely nullified by the most intolerable obscurities and contradictions imaginable.

In the final paragraph of page 355, Stammler makes the following claim about "knowledge of nature." It always proceeds "from one cause" and traces it back "to a *higher* cause." "The former cause is the *effect* of the latter." In other words, Stammler reifies natural laws as "causally effective forces." On the other hand, five pages before this (Stammler, p. 350), Stammler provides a comprehensive discussion of the following thesis: causality is not an "intrinsically necessary" connection. On the contrary, it is only "a conceptual element, a basic, unifying concept within the domain of our knowledge." At the bottom of p. 351, Stammler claims that "experience" can only provide knowledge of the contents of "perception insofar as it is ordered according to uniform axioms" (*"for example"*—note!—"the law of causality"). And on p. 371, he also represents causality as an *"example"* of the empirical, "indubitable, general *concepts*" (!) which have a regulative status in relation to knowledge. Finally, on page 368 Stammler claims that there is *"only one kind of scientific* knowledge of concrete phenomena," namely causal knowledge.[25] Of course these views are clearly inconsistent with the claims he makes on pages 378–379. On p. 378, he refers to a "teleological *science*," and on p. 379 he refers to "human purposes which have a regulative function in relation to *science*." On p. 378, "teleological science" is differentiated from "natural science." In this context, therefore, "natural science" must be equivalent to "causal" knowledge. On p. 350, Stammler describes causality as the fundamental category of *every* "empirical science." Therefore it presumably follows that *no* "teleological science" is an empirical science. How is the distinction between "teleological" and "natural" science established? Does Stammler offer the simple answer that they represent two completely different *problematics*? Does he then provide an exposition and a logical analysis of these two problematics? No. He responds to this question with a chaos of mistaken assertions that are almost totally useless.

On p. 352, Stammler claims that the following "are included in the contents of our ideas": "the idea of making *choices* and the idea of performing actions." Fine. The existence of *ideas* of this sort is a fact of everyday inner experience which no one would deny. What follows from this fact?

"Why," asks Stammler, "must this ideational content be an *illusion*?" Let me make the following point parenthetically. It is obvious that, from the standpoint of determinism, this "ideational content" is *not* an "illusion" at all. It is an absolute empirical certainty that a man's ability to treat his own conduct as an object of conscious deliberation exercises an overwhelming influence upon the way he actually behaves. It is obvious that the actor, in order to be *capable* of acting, does not require the idea that his conduct is *not* "determined." Nor does the representation of his conduct as an unequivocally determined process transform the idea of "choice" into an "illusion." Just to the contrary. From a "psychological" point of view, a "struggle" *has* indeed taken place between the ideational purposes of which he is aware, purposes that he sees as "possibilities." Finally, suppose that the actor holds deterministic beliefs about his choices. This supposition does not entail that such an act of choice can be causally explained as an act that is "idiosyncratic," a consequence of the actor's *own* authentic personal characteristics, a result of his (empirically) "constant motives." On the contrary, the actor does not enter the theater of "illusion" until he commits himself to an "indeterminist" metaphysics. This happens when he claims that his conduct is "free" in the sense of being completely or partially "indeterminate." Stammler himself is committed to just this sort of metaphysics. In view of the passages cited (Stammler, pp. 351–352), there is no doubt at all that we can ascribe the following view to Stammler. Suppose that, in spite of the presence of the idea of "choice," the action which is "to be brought about by the actor himself" is conceived as *determined*. Then, according to Stammler, that idea of "choice" would indeed be an "illusion." As Stammler already claims on page 344, this would be inconsistent with the concept of "choice." This concept, according to Stammler, excludes the possibility of "an unequivocally binding causality." However Stammler obscures and limits the exact meaning of this proposition on pages 344-345, where he makes the following claim. There is "no doubt" that "in the vast *majority* of cases" we *also* include among the "results" of future human actions "those *consequences that might not have occurred*."

In Stammler's view, this position is not inconsistent with the unconditional validity of the basic axiom of all experience (Stammler, p. 352). His reasons are the following. (1) As long as a "choice" between them remains open, actions do not *yet* qualify as empirical facts. They are only "possibilities." But precisely the same point could be made concerning any "natural process": for example, a fight between two animals as long as the outcome is still in doubt. (2) The problem of "correct" choice—in other words, the problem of the choice which *should be* made—does not lie within the domain of "natural science" (Stammler, p. 352). Naturally this latter thesis is quite obviously true. However its truth would be very much in doubt if it were dependent upon the validity of Stammler's argument concerning the actor's process of "choosing" and the limits of causal inquiry. That argument is completely irrelevant to this "question of value." Moreover it is obvious that this argument is *not* valid. I can find a sunset "beautiful" and a rainy day "dreadful," and I can judge an opinion to be "fallacious" even though I am convinced that the circumstances of each case are causally determined. Both "instinctive" consumption and the most sophisticated fare can be evaluated from the standpoint of their dietetic "utility." Further, the following question can be raised about any human "action" and any natural process. How did it transpire (in the past) "so that" successful results were assured? Or how "*must*" it transpire (in the future) "so that" successful results will be assured? The medical doctor is invariably obliged to pose this question (implicitly). Depending upon his own behavior, the "rational" actor may see that his conduct has several "possible" results. Further, he may have in mind several different "maxims" which may function as the determining motives of his choices. Therefore his action is "inhibited" until this internal "struggle" is resolved. From an empirical standpoint, this is undoubtedly one of the fundamentally important modalities of "mental processes."

Consider, however, the analysis of these processes, processes in which the idea of one or more possible "results" is among the causal determinants of human conduct. Note that this idea of one or more possible "results" is invariably only *one* of the determinants. It is obvious that such an analysis does not transcend the limits of a causal inquiry. Consider the process by which a "choice" is made between several "purposes" each of which is conceived as "possible." Suppose that this process is subjected to an *empirical* inquiry. Now consider this process from beginning to end, including all the rational deliberations and moral ideas which enter into its formation. This process can be conceived as strictly determined, in exactly the same sense that any "natural phenomenon" is conceived as strictly determined. Stammler never denies this explicitly. In page after page of circumlocution, however, he circles around the point. In one passage (Stammler, p. 368), he says that "freedom cannot be ascribed to the *performance*" of an action. Does this mean that freedom can be ascribed "to the intention"? Shortly thereafter he identifies "experience" with the concept of the "observable." Since mental processes are not "observable," the reader remains in doubt concerning the question of their determination. On page 341, Stammler explicitly claims that "the idea of something which a human being brings about" does not fall within the domain of "observation" (the domain which he identifies with "nature" on p. 378).[26] This only makes the status of mental processes even more obscure. And he adds to these considerations the argument (see Stammler, p. 352, a passage we have already cited) that "future" events which are conceived as "possibilities" do not really qualify as "empirical facts." Stammler even makes the explicit claim that the progression of causes does not have the same *logical* status as the retrogression of causes: experience is possible only concerning *the past* (Stammler, p. 346). *Therefore* experience remains "incomplete" and "inconclusive." Several other miscellaneous claims are added to this argument in a confused fashion. Stammler says that experience is not "omniscient." It does not encompass "the totality of human insight" (Stammler, p. 346). Therefore it provides no basis for a relationship between the knowing subject and the object of knowledge. Experience is said to be valid (Stammler, p. 347) only within the limits of its "formal axioms" (?). *Therefore* experience is not a source of "eternal truths" of "timeless validity." In consequence, it cannot claim to have "absolute *value*." On the other hand, consider the passage on page 345 discussed above. At that point, it is only "most" future actions that fail to qualify as necessary.

And so the obscurity of Stammler's text is perpetuated. Questions of every conceivable sort are posed, only to be confused with one another. Stammler considers the possibility of "*conceiving*" (note!) an action as one which is "brought about by the actor." But we do not know whether this is the conception of the actor himself or the conception of the "observer" for whom the action is an *object* of knowledge. This possibility is *distinguished* from the possibility of conceiving the action as "causally determined" (Stammler, bottom of p. 357 and top of p. 358). At the same time, however, the following reservation is introduced concerning the latter possibility. It is *limited* by the consideration that there is still "no single, indubitable law of nature which comprehends the causal necessity of future human actions, a law which would have a status similar to the status of the law of gravity." And even if the situation were "improved" (!), it would not follow that "*all* human conduct" would "conform" (!) to this law. Suppose that our "nomological" knowledge were absolutely exhaustive. Does Stammler think that the "totality" of (extra-human) *natural* phenomena could ever be deduced and "computed" from such a set of laws? Stammler does not even have a fragmentary grasp of the relationship between "law" and "concrete case" and the general epistemological significance of the irrationality of reality. Occasionally he acknowledges that *actual* gaps in "experience," even though they may be very large, are of no *logical* relevance at all. On the other hand, he goes on to employ this idea of the incompleteness of experience. As a result, the "kingdom of ends" is invariably degraded to an ad hoc status. Yet Stammler also ascribes a distinctive *epistemological* significance to the "kingdom of ends." But suppose we conclude this dismal analysis and briefly set out what Stammler *could* have had in mind.

In order to understand Stammler's view of the distinction between "natural science" and "social science," we shall have to identify another concept of "nature." But before we pursue Stammler's own views any further, let us employ the analyses undertaken in the foregoing section and attempt to clarify the possibilities that lie open.

As we have seen, Stammler conceives "publicly observable" norms as the "form," the "presupposition," the "epistemological condition," of "social life" and knowledge of "social life." In our discussion of the concept of a rule of a game,^{27} we considered the various possible meanings of these repeated assertions—assertions that Stammler expresses in constantly varying language—in order to ascribe some intelligible sense to them. At this point let us draw some conclusions from this discussion. First consider the following possibility. "Knowledge" of "social life" is *no more or less than* an "evaluation" of "social life." It is *only* conceivable as the search for an "ideal" and a "socio*political*" *evaluation* of the actual condition of social life by reference to this ideal standard. We shall not take this possibility into account. On the contrary, we shall assume that Stammler's purpose is to define the object of an *empirical* science, an object for which "publicly observable" (legal and "conventional") *norms* constitute a "presupposition."

Stammler's Concept of "Social Life"

The second book of Stammler's work is entitled "The Object of Social Science." As we have seen, its purpose is to develop a certain concept of "social life." Given Stammler's intentions, both (Rümelin's) concept of "society" and the concept of the state should be subordinated to this concept. This concept of "social life" should also be logically related to the concept of a "rule." Even in the first passage in which Stammler introduces this concept (Stammler, p. 83, line 15), however, the following ambiguities appear. The factor which constitutes "social life as a distinctive object of our knowledge" is alleged to be "the order which originates in human conduct, intercourse, and communal life." This is expressed even more clearly on page 85, where Stammler uses the expression: a "norm which emanates from men." What does this mean? Let us examine the following possibilities. Consider the "rule" in which the concept of "social life" is anchored. (I) It could mean that this "rule" is (1) instituted as an "obligatory norm," or is (2) followed as a maxim. Or it could mean that the "rule" (3) must satisfy both of these conditions. These possibilities raise the following question: Is it necessary for the rule to be a "maxim" which actual men really employ? (II) Or is it sufficient that "*we*"—the observers—"conceive" a reciprocal relationship between men who coexist within certain spatio-temporal coordinates as subject to a "rule"? This "conception" could have two different senses. (1) We could "abstract" or "derive" a "rule" from the reciprocal relationship. In other words, we see the relationship as empirically rule-governed. (2) Or we could see the relationship in a very different sense, a sense that we have already discussed extensively. From "our" standpoint, the standpoint of the observer, it seems that a "norm"—and note that this is an "ideal norm"—can apply or must apply to the relationship.

Stammler would certainly repudiate possibility II.1 (the "rule" as empirical regularity). It is obviously inconsistent with his intentions. A "rule" is to be understood as an "imperative," not as an empirical regularity. In fact, Stammler—in reply to a remark by Kistiakowski and very much on his high horse—finds it incomprehensible that anyone who had read his book could even raise this question.[28] Really? Then what does it mean when Stammler persistently speaks as if collective human life and its reciprocal relationships would be reduced to "turmoil," "chaos," and "confusion"— he also uses other expressions of this sort—by a purely empirical-causal inquiry?[29] Finally, in light of his response to Kistiakowski, consider Stammler's remarks on page 641. Here he makes it explicit that an inquiry into human relations which does *not* employ the concept of a "rule" as an "imperative" has *no* place in his discussion of "social life." The *isolated* existence of the "single man being," Stammler claims (Stammler, p. 84), constitutes the "objective" or "substantive" polar antithesis of "societal" life. Moreover he makes it quite explicit that the "single human being" is the hypothetical primitive man who lives in utter isolation.

How is it possible for Stammler to make these claims? Is is not obvious that the polar antithesis of "societal life" could only be identified in something like the following way (for the present, we shall not worry over the precise formulation of this point): it is constituted by "those relationships that men have to 'nature' and to one another which do *not* fall under 'man-made rules'" (in the imperative sense of this expression)? Of course this is an aspect of Stammler's style that is already quite familiar to us. However it is astonishing that in the passage under discussion (Stammler, p. 84), he suddenly begins to speak of "objective" or "substantive" distinctions and not of "conceptual" or "logical" distinctions, as he did on page 77 and elsewhere. At the top of p. 87, on the other hand, he identifies a "substantive" or "objective" distinction with a "conceptual" or "logical" distinction. Variations in the purpose of the inquiry and differences in the empirically "established" facts, therefore, are treated as if they were equivalent. (1) Suppose that Stammler's intention is to provide a "logical" definition of a specific "object of knowledge" by describing the definitive *purpose* of the inquiry into this object. If this is the case, then it is obvious that the following must be excluded from the domain of "social life" as Stammler conceives it: "*all* relationships which men have with one another and with 'nature' " *insofar as* they are conceived purely empirically, and not as ideally possible cases of the application of "rules" (in the imperative sense). It follows that "social life" is not a possible object of investigation within the empirical-causal sciences. It can only be an object of inquiry for a "dogmatic" science. (2) Suppose, on the other hand, that Stammler's purpose is to provide an "objective" definition of certain aspects of empirical reality that are found within the world of empirically given "objects." Such an ostensive definition would be based on the distinctive qualitative features which can actually be identified in those aspects of reality included under the definition. In this case, it is obvious that the ("objective") polar antithesis to Stammler's concept of "social life" must be identified as follows. It includes "*all* human conduct" in relation to "nature" and to other men which satisfies at least one of the following two conditions. *In fact*, the actors in question have not "instituted" a constitutive "norm" as obligatory for this sort of conduct (see I.1 above). Or (see I.2 and I.3 above) *in fact* the actors in question do not follow this sort of "norm" as a "maxim." Therefore the issue of whether something is a "natural process" or a phenomenon of "social life" is dependent upon the answers to the following questions. To what extent does it in fact agree with a "precept" (see I.1)?[30] Or to what extent (see I.3) do the actors in question in fact make self-conscious positive or negative commitments concerning these "precepts"? Or finally (see I.2), in spite of the absence of an explicit "precept," to what extent does the idea of obligatory norms for observable human behavior influence human conduct in a concrete case, at least subjectively? Or to what extent is this idea at least concomitant with the conduct in question?

It would be pointless to try to find unambiguous answers to these questions in Stammler's work. That characteristic "style of imprecision" which we discussed in the foregoing makes it possible for Stammler to evade the responsibility for providing these answers. In this case, the technique of evasion is a very simple one. The "rule" is *personified* and employed in a purely "metaphorical" sense. On pages 98-99, Stammler discusses the "publicly observable rule"—in contrast to the moral norm, which requires "conviction." At this point, Stammler defines a "publicly observable rule" as a rule "the meaning of which (note!) is completely independent of the motive which the individual has for following it."[31] The metaphor, therefore, should be interpreted as follows: the "publicly observable rule" is defined by reference to its ideal, dogmatically deducible "validity." This view of the "publicly observable rule" emerges even more clearly in the following passage (Stammler, p. 99, line 9, *seq.*). Stammler explicitly claims that the question of the status of "the rule" is "irrelevant" to the following issue. Has "the person subject to the rule reflected upon it at all"? Or does he simply follow the rule as a result of "indifferent habituation"? Presumably this also means that the question of the status of "the rule" is irrelevant to the question of whether the person is even acquainted with the rule. Or is this the case? Consider also an empirically precise distinction between pragmatic action consciously oriented to norms and all other conduct. From the standpoint of such a distinction, it is obvious that the rule which is followed because of "indifferent habituation" and the rule which is followed because of animal "instincts" would be indistinguishable.

Stammler, very cleverly, has nothing at all to say about the case in which the "rule" is *not* in fact followed. Only an account of this case would make it possible to establish exactly what it is that Stammler has in mind at this point. However such an account would also establish conclusively that the question of whether or not a rule is in fact followed is irrelevant to the question of the ideal (dogmatic) "validity" of the rule. If Stammler had employed these standards of precision, then it would obviously have been impossible for him to use the following scholastic device (see Stammler, p. 100). Because the (personified) rule "can be distinguished . . . from the motives (note!) that are characteristic of the isolated (!) man," this rule appears "as a new, independent determinant (note!) of human conduct" (note that on pp. 98-99 Stammler claims that the rule "appears as independent of the motives which the individual person has for following the rule"). On pages 98-99, Stammler claims that the (empirical) determinant (or, as Stammler puts it, the "motive") is *irrelevant* to observable behavior. The "rule"—as Stammler expresses it—"is independent of the motive." If the metaphorical trappings are stripped away, this point only amounts to the following. In the normative evaluation of conduct, *we* abstract or bracket[32] the actual motivation of the actor and only consider the legality of his observable behavior. At this point (Stammler, p. 100), the "isolated" man is suddenly and surreptitiously introduced as the polar antithesis of "social life." And just as suddenly, the ideal "validity" of a norm as a standard of *evaluation* which *we*, the observers, employ is given a familiar turn. It is interpreted as an empirical determinant of human action. At the top of page 99, Stammler considers the possibility that the person who follows the norm (ideally) submits to it self-consciously because of his moral or formal-legal convictions. He says that this is a completely irrelevant possibility. But now (on p. 100) it is represented as an empirical fact, the definitive criterion of "collective life as governed by publicly observable rules."

It is quite obvious that this sleight of hand is made possible in the following way.[33] The unsuspecting reader learns that "the rule *presents itself as* independent of the motive" which the person has for following it. However this point remains obscure. In one kind of case, *we*—the inquirers—are engaged in a "dogmatic" inquiry. Therefore we regard "the rule" as having ideal *axiological* validity, and we bracket or abstract the actual motivation of the actor. In the other kind of case, however, we are concerned with empirical knowledge. Actual men are included among the *objects* of our knowledge. By instituting a rule, they attempt to achieve an actual "goal." And in general—with varying degrees of certainty—they really succeed. Stammler, in order to insure that his scholastic obscurities will remain utterly impenetrable, personifies the "law of nature" and represents it as parallel to the "precept" (see Stammler, p. 100, line 23). They are distinguished in the following way. The purpose of the "precept" is to "constitute" a certain collective life. The purpose of the "law of nature," therefore, is to "*cognitively* (*sic!*) constitute" empirical regularity as "the unity of natural phenomena." The idea of a rule which "wants, means, or intends" something is at least a logically possible metaphor. In this context, of course, it is absolutely impermissible. However the idea of a rule that "thinks" or performs "acts of cognition" is utterly absurd.

In view of the extensive analysis undertaken in the foregoing section of this essay, further criticism of this point is presumably unnecessary. Therefore it would be superfluous to devote an independent critique to Stammler's reasoning in pp. 100-105. Consider the rule which is described as an "independent" (empirical) "determinant" of action on p. 100. At the bottom of p. 101, it again becomes a "formally definitive element" of a *concept*. Then at the middle of p. 102, it becomes an "epistemological condition" for the "possibility" of the concept of "social life." Finally on p. 105—when it is obviously too late—Stammler exhorts the reader as follows: on no account should "a *causal* consequence be inferred from the *logical* function (!) of observable rules." As we have seen, this is precisely the inference that Stammler himself makes a few pages earlier. Consider his own admonition: that logical-conceptual and empirical-objective relationships should not be conflated. This is the more general formulation of the import of the distinction that Stammler has in mind. Stammler fails to heed his own exhortation, even in the discussion which immediately follows it (see Stammler, p. 105). At this point, the *concept* of "social life" and—as Stammler calls it—the *concept* of "isolated" life are represented as constituting a rigorous and mutually exclusive dichotomy. At least this is how we shall interpret this passage for the present. It follows that there are no real, empirical *facts* which resist exhaustive subsumption under one of these two concepts. It is invariably the case that a given fact falls under one and only one of these two concepts (note!). "A third possibility is quite inconceivable."

Let us examine this reasoning in more detail. What are the only two "conceivable" kinds of fact? On the one hand, "the single (note!) man who dwells (note!) in complete isolation." On the other hand, "life in association with others that is subject to publicly observable rules." Stammler thinks that these two alternatives are absolutely exhaustive, so completely exhaustive that "evolution" is only possible "within one of these two states." "Evolution" from the state of "isolation" to the state of "social life" is alleged to be impossible. It is "conceptually" impossible, as Stammler adds, quite casually and in the style that we know so well. Then he goes on to illustrate this point with the case of Robinson Crusoe.[34] This particular sleight of hand is produced in the following way. Consider those "precepts" by reference to which a plurality of men are associated. Stammler himself habitually employs this expression "precept." In the interest of clarity, we shall use it too. In this decisive passage, the reader is given the impression that the distinction is only concerned with a plurality of men associated by these "precepts," on the one hand, and *one* absolutely isolated individual, on the other. But in many other passages, Stammler himself refers to *several* coexisting individuals whose relationships are not regulated by "precepts." Therefore "precepts" do not qualify as a "determinant" of their reciprocal conduct.

From Stammler's point of view, therefore, this latter state of affairs would be conceptually equivalent to the circumstances of the "isolated dweller." At this point, however, Stammler makes another surreptitious move. He considers a kind of coexistence that is not governed by "precepts." He calls it "purely physical." In his view it is no different from a society of animals. This gives the reader the following impression. There is only one possible polar antithesis to "social life." It is a purely spatio-temporal coexistence that excludes all other relationships. But in other passages Stammler provides a detailed discussion of the predominant influence of pure "instincts," "drives," and so on—in other words, "psychological" factors—within this purely spatio-temporal coexistence. In one passage, the explicit emphasis on the "instinctual" leads the reader to believe that Stammler is talking about the state of unconscious torpor. But at this point still another covert move is made. In Defoe's work, Robinson Crusoe's "economy" is certainly not "instinctual." On the contrary, it is a product of teleological "rationality." According to Stammler, however (Stammler, p. 105), Robinson's "economy" does not lie within the domain of "conduct subject to publicly observable rules," but rather within the domain of "pure technique." If Stammler were consistent on this point, he would find himself committed to the following position. Consider Robinson's purposive action "in relation to" others. Suppose he has the conscious intention to influence the conduct of someone in a systematic fashion. This sort of conduct does not lie within the domain of "social life" because it is not governed by "prescriptive" *norms.*

We have already clarified the "logical" consequences of this position. At this juncture we only want to make one further point. In at least one passage (Stammler, pp. 101-102), Stammler himself recognizes these logical consequences. In another passage, of course (Stammler, pp. 96-97), he again introduces reservations: even the use of language constitutes a "conventional regulation" of human conduct. Therefore the use of language qualifies as social life. It is certainly true that every use of "language" is an "interpretive technique," a means of reaching an "understanding." But as such, it does not amount to an understanding of precepts. Nor does it rest on "precepts." Stammler, however, claims that the use of language does rest upon precepts. His reason is the following. The grammar of a language is a set of *prescriptive rules*. Their "acquisition" "is supposed to bring" about behavior of a certain sort. As regards the relationship between a pupil in the sixth form and his teacher, this is quite correct. In order to make *this* sort of "acquisition" of language possible, it was necessary for "grammarians" to transform the *empirical* regularities of linguistic use into a system of *norms*, a system the maintenance of which is enforced by pedagogical discipline: the teacher's paddle. At the bottom of p. 97, however, Stammler himself claims that a "totally isolated coexistence" is conceivable only if we abstract from it any sort of "agreement" in "language and *conduct*" (note!).

At this point Stammler is obliged to answer for the covert maneuver that is responsible for the antithesis between "collective life regulated by precepts" and "total isolation." The last remark cited in the foregoing paragraph is correct. But consider its implications. On the one hand, the mere *fact* of "agreement" or "consensus" must be a sufficient condition for the constitution of "social life." The question of whether this consensus is a causal result of a "precept," an involuntary physical reaction, a "reflex," a process of "deliberation," "instinct," and so on is irrelevant. Therefore, in spite of all that Stammler claims in pp. 87-95, it is not even possible for animals to live a *non*social life unless—given Stammler's own definitional concepts—all agreement in their "conduct" breaks down completely. Since "interpretive techniques" or "means for reaching an understanding" include everything that falls under Stammler's concept of agreement in "conduct," this point can be stated more generally as follows: a *non*social life is possible for animals only if all their "means for reaching an understanding" break down completely. Finally, it follows that men lead a social life if it can be demonstrated that they in fact employ "interpretive techniques" or "means for reaching an understanding." The question of how these techniques were produced is irrelevant. Therefore the question of whether they are a product of "human precepts" is also irrelevant.

However this is surely not Stammler's position. On p. 106, he makes a claim that is incompatible—even inconsistent— with this position. "Social life," he claims, exists *only* where a "precept" has been *established*. This claim is made explicit in the following rather naïve statement. "Suppose someone wants . . . to transport his imagination into another period of human existence. Since an impulse to association under publicly observable rules evolves . . . *gradually* (note!) in the human spirit . . . everything (note!) depends upon the point in time at which these precepts (note!) were originally developed (!). From that point on we have social life. Before that point we do not. An intermediate stage . . . makes no sense" (!).[35] Of course this is nothing new. The scholastic jurist can conceive the possibility of "social life" only in the form of a civil compact. But exactly how "genuine" is Stammler's scholasticism? We find out at the top of p. 107. "Evolution" and "conceptual transition" are conflated. Therefore by establishing the *logical* impossibility of the latter—and, indeed, simply because of the *linguistic* pairing, "conceptual transition" is a patent absurdity—Stammler also believes he had established the *empirical* impossibility of the former.

Therefore let us suppose that such a "transition" is "inconceivable." In that case, the following question becomes absolutely critical. What is the definitive *criterion* for the ultimate origin—or, more generally, the existence—of a "precept"? Since savages are not in the habit of drafting legal codes, presumably there could only be one answer to this question. The criterion is human behavior which is (in legal terms) "conclusive" for the existence of a norm. But when is this condition satisfied? Only if the norm is included among the ideas of the men in question? In other words, only if at least one of the following conditions if satisfied: either they live—in a subjectively intentional fashion—according to the "normative" maxim; or, if they violate it, they do so with the knowledge that their conduct is in "violation" of a norm. According to Stammler, however, the internal subjective attitude toward the legal norm—even knowledge of the norm itself—is supposed to be irrelevant to the existence of the norm. "Indifferent habituation," in his view, has the same consequences as the self-conscious "normative maxim." What, therefore, are we obliged to conclude?

Perhaps the criterion for the identification of a "precept" is the following: it can be observed that men act *as if* a precept existed. But under what conditions is this the case? Consider the mother who breast feeds her child. In the "Prussian General Code of Provincial Law," this task is a legal responsibility of the mother. Therefore it falls within the domain of "social life" as Stammler defines it. But in general the Prussian mother who nurses her child knows nothing at all about this "norm." Her knowledge on this point is comparable to the knowledge of a mother among the Australian aborigines. She does the same thing with at least the same regularity. And she has no idea that breast feeding is *not* an obligation enjoined by "publicly observable rules." Therefore it follows that, according to Stammler, breast feeding among the Australian aborigines is *not* part of the "social life" of that society. It could not even be said that a "conventional norm" of breast feeding exists in this case. The claim that a "conventional norm" exists in a case of this sort would simply mean the following: a certain degree of purely empirical "regularity" in behavior can be confirmed. Of course it is quite often true that—again, from a subjective point of view—"conventional" normative ideas actually "evolve" as consequences of purely empirical regularities. The following are among the sources of these "conventional" normative ideas: an uncertain fear of deviating from traditional behavior; the distaste and aversion this fear produces on the part of those who encounter a deviation from traditional behavior; the fear that gods or men whose interests (conceived in purely egoistic terms) could be violated by such a deviation from traditional behavior might take revenge. Moreover the idea of a "duty" to observe a norm that is, from a purely empirical standpoint, "customary" may develop from a fear of conduct that is "uncommon" or "exceptional." And the purely instinctive or egoistic aversion to "innovation" and "novelty" may develop into a "condemnation" of these same things.

But does this subjective behavior imply the idea of a "precept"? In a given concrete case, it is quite obvious that this issue would often remain problematical. But consider Stammler's position. The "subjective" fact and the actor's "conviction" are completely *irrelevant* as criteria for the identification of a "precept." It follows that there are no empirical criteria for the identification of "precepts." The "observable" behavior remains the same, regardless of whether a "precept" is present (see the above case of breast feeding). And suppose that "observable" behavior gradually changes under the influence of the development of "normative" ideas. In that case, the issue of whether the empirical existence of "publicly observable" ("conventional" or "legal") norms should be inferred from this change is merely a matter of opinion.

Given Stammler's conceptual scheme, it is obviously absurd to suppose that a purposeful and self-conscious "impulse" to institute "precepts" could ever develop in the "spirit" of the primitive man who "lives in total isolation" (note!). Therefore let us consider a question that Stammler himself raises, and let us pose it in his "style." How, in general, is it possible to conceive the empirical origins of "social life" in an animal-like herd? There is only one possible answer to this question. The origin of social life is simply not conceivable as a temporal, empirical process. "Social life" is—as we might put it—"transtemporal."[36] Any answer to this question which employs the *concept* "man" is obviously not a solution to an empirical problem. On the contrary, it is an exercise in mystification.

This may be explained as follows. Suppose we believe that it is logically possible to establish a certain "concept" of "social life." And suppose that, given this belief, we draw the following conclusion: If a given, real, empirical fact corresponds to this concept of social life, then this fact could develop in only one way—as a "realization" of this concept. Any alternative is impossible. In other words, we conclude that actual men simply had to see the "realization" of this "concept" as the aim of their conduct. Given this problematic, mystification is the inevitable path of retreat. Now suppose that this naïve pragmatic is rejected. Consider the hypothetical notion of a "gradual" awakening of "normative ideas": the awakening of a belief that (in Stammler's own words) certain actions—performed in "indifferent habituation," performed "instinctively" throughout countless ages without any thought at all of "obligation" or even "precept"—are "duties." Suppose that the awakening of this belief is accompanied by the vague fear that the neglect of these "duties" could prove to be harmful. This hypothetical idea poses no substantive difficulties. In this sense, even a dog has a "feeling of duty." But consider Stammler's idea that "duties" of this sort rest on "human precepts." In contrast to "ethics," "only an external legality" can be ascribed to them (Stammler, p. 98). Conceptually, this is sheer rubbish. Moreover even our most rudimentary "historical" evidence—in the usual sense of this expression—shows that Stammler's idea on this point is mistaken.

Consider the claim that the (empirical) existence of a "precept" is a necessary condition for the occurrence of a process in the world of human conduct. Suppose that the domain of "social life" is circumscribed in this fashion. In that case, this domain is constantly subject to variations that are a result of the gradual transformation of pure facticities into processes "regulated by external rules." And suppose that, following Stammler, "conventions" are included in the class of "precepts." The same point still holds. This is a process of transition that occurs repeatedly. Stammler employs a deliberately precautionary subterfuge at this point (Stammler, pp. 106-107). He says that this process of transition only amounts to an evolution of the "content" of social life. This sort of evolution, therefore, presupposes the existence of social life itself. It is obvious that this proves nothing at all concerning the *inconceivability* of such a "transition." This is because the same kind of evolution is in principle possible for *all* aspects of "social life" as Stammler conceives it. From an empirical standpoint, moreover, the concept of *"external"* or *"observable"* "norms" as a criterion for "social" life—in contrast to the "moral" life—is utterly useless. Even a "primitive" ethics makes an unconditional claim to "external" legality. It is never possible to make a precise empirical distinction between "primitive" ethics, on the one hand, and "law" and "convention," on the other. From the standpoint of primitive "normative ideas," norms are not "man-made." Just to the contrary. Whenever the question of the origin of a norm arises, the usual primitive response is that the norm is a divine "decree." Of course the question of the origins of the individual components of our contemporary concepts of "law" and "legal norm" would pose extraordinary difficulties for the ethnographer. Perhaps reliable historical knowledge concerning the solution to such a problem will remain *empirically* inaccessible. Nevertheless, confronted with difficulties of this sort, the ethnographer will certainly not adopt the ludicrous role of the scholastic jurist. There is only one simple-minded question which the scholastic is obliged to pose concerning the phenomena of primitive life. Does the process in question fall under the category of external, publicly observable rules? In other words, is it subject to human precepts (in the sense of Stammler's *Economy and Law*, p. 77, *seq.*)? Or is it a case of purely instinctual collective life (in the sense of Stammler, p. 87, *seq.*)? It must be one of the two. Otherwise it could not be classified within my conceptual scheme. And if that were the case, the result would be dreadful: the process would be "inconceivable."

Stammler misconceives the "significance" of concept formation and conceptual schemes. Therefore he constantly confuses the knower and the known, the knowing subject and the object of knowledge. Let us conclude our discussion of this doctrine by examining the following intriguing gloss (see Stammler, p. 91) on the concept (note!) of "social life" which we encounter (!) in experience (note!). "Empirically given (note!) social life rests" (presumably this can only mean: empirically) "on external rules" (as we know, this is ambiguous). "These rules" (which must mean: this *fact*) "make social life comprehensible as a special concept (!) and as an independent object" (in other words, it is a "concept" which becomes "comprehensible"). "This is because we see in them (namely, the 'rules'—this is ambiguous) the possibility . . . of understanding a human relationship (note!) that is essentially independent of the mere discovery (!) of the properties of the instinctual life of the single individual" (in other words, it is an empirical *fact*—a "human relationship"—which is empirically "independent" of our *knowledge* of certain other empirical facts). Again I say: Enough of this confusion. In order to unravel every thread of the net of sophisms in which Stammler· has enmeshed his reader—and, more important, himself—it would be necessary to consider literally every proposition in the book, analyze its internal inconsistencies, and determine the respects in which it is inconsistent with other claims Stammler makes.

At this point, let us only identify the error which is the source of Stammler's foolish claim about the "inconceivablility" of a "transition." Suppose we set up a distinction between the "ideal" *axiological* validity of a "norm," on the one hand, and some purely "empirical" *fact,* on the other— for example, the actual conduct of a real person. This dichotomy does indeed exclude the possibility of any "transition." It is obviously and utterly irreconcilable. Any "mediation" between the two poles of the dichotomy is conceptually "inconceivable." Why? The reason is extremely simple. The two poles of the dichotomy identify two completely different *problematics* and two completely different cognitive purposes. One is concerned with a dogmatic inquiry into the ideal "meaning" of a "precept" and the "*evaluation*" of empirical action by reference to this standard. The other is concerned with the identification of empirical action as a "fact" and the causal "explanation" of this fact. Consider this point of *logic.* There are two different, theoretically possible "problematics" by reference to which an inquiry may be conducted. Stammler projects this property of knowledge onto empirical reality. This is the source of that piece of nonsense about the "conceptual" impossibility of a "transition" in empirical reality. The confusion that Stammler introduces within the domain of logic is no less serious. Here we find the inverse error. From a *logical* point of view, the two problematics are absolutely different. Yet Stammler constantly conflates them.

As a result of this conflation, Stammler places insuperable obstacles in the path of his own self-appointed task: the definition of the domain and the problems of "social science." This is obvious if we examine the concluding remarks at the end of the first section of Book Two (Stammler, p. 107, seq.). At this point Stammler discusses the principle of his own problematic. "In contrast to the (!) science of nature," "social science" must "proceed in accordance with its own definitive properties." This obviously means that "social science" is to be distinguished from "the science of nature." Stammler regards the "status" (!−he should have said "object," in the sense of "nature" or "essence") of "natural science" as "philosophically secure" (Stammler, p. 107). Really? It is well known that in the logical discussions of the last ten years no issue is more controversial than this problem. In earlier sections of this essay,[37] we identified no less than four different possible concepts of "nature." None of them, however, qualifies as the polar antithesis of what Stammler calls "collective life governed by external rules."

Consider the concepts of nature which juxtapose one part of empirically given reality to another part. In the final analysis, this latter part is constituted by the so-called "higher" human functions. But according to Stammler, the entire domain of norms that are "exclusively" concerned with "inner," moral conduct is *not included* under this concept of "collective life governed by external rules." That is why none of these concepts of nature can serve as the polar antithesis of Stammler's concept of "social life." Consider also the distinction which identifies the domain of "nature" as the domain of the "meaningless" and differentiates it from objects which are identified by reference to their "meaning." This distinction is also useless as a polar antithesis of "social life" as Stammler conceives it. The reason: Not all the objects to which a "meaning" can be ascribed fall under Stammler's concept of "collective life governed by external rules." Not even all "meaningful" human conduct falls under this concept. The logical distinction between knowledge in the "natural sciences" as general (nomothetic) and knowledge in the historical sciences as concrete or individual has no place at all in Stammler's problematic. Consider, therefore, the different possible imports of the expression "natural science" which have been discussed thus far. It seems that only one possibility remains: "Natural scientific" knowledge in the sense of "empirical"–and therefore non"dogmatic"–knowledge and a concept of "nature" the extension of which would correspond to this kind of knowledge. But "social science" as Stammler conceives it is not supposed to be the same as jurisprudence. Nor, obviously, is it supposed to be a science that investigates "conventional" rules from the standpoint of jurisprudence. Therefore it is obvious that this distinction is of no consequence either.

All *practical* problems could be called "sociopolitical" (in the broadest sense of this expression) insofar as they pose the following question: According to what "legal" or "conventional" norms *should* observable human behavior be regulated? Suppose that our purpose is to identify an *empirical* science in such a way that it constitutes the polar antithesis of this complex of practical problems. And suppose that, following Stammler, we christen it "social science" and call its subject matter "social life." In that case, the domain of "social life" would have to be defined in the following way. It includes all empirical processes which satisfy the following condition: the "external" or "observable" normative regulation of these processes in accordance with "human precepts" is "in principle"–without objective contradictions–*conceivable*. At this point the question of whether such a definition of the concept of "social life" has any scientific "value" at all is irrelevant. We are only concerned with the following requirements. The definition should be internally consistent, and it should not compromise the purely empirical status of its object: "social life." At the same time, its import should include everything that Stammler could have intended, if he had actually understood his own work "correctly." The definition should at least make it logically and empirically possible to *define* the object by reference to "external rules": "rule" *not* in the sense of empirical facticity, but rather in the sense of "idea." It should eliminate the confusion between the ideal "validity" of the "rule" and the empirical "existence" of the "rule." Finally, this would also dispose of the following misconceived idea. "Social life," thus defined, constitutes a peculiar "universe of purposes" or some other universe of objects that satisfy the following condition: *although* they exist empirically, they are not possible objects of a causal investigation.

Notes

1. The book discussed here is Rudolf Stammler, *Wirtschaft und Recht nach der materialistischen Geschichtsauffassung: Eine sozialphilosophische Untersuchung*, 2nd edition, revised (Leipzig: Veit and Company, 1906).

2. In the interests of coherence, the ensuing critique is written in such a way that the points made—some of them quite elementary—are apparently stated for the first time. As regards some of these points, it is obvious that this is absolutely not the case. Although this point will not escape the scholar, I want to note it explicitly. Views of earlier critics of Stammler will also be discussed.

3. See Stammler, p. 63, *seq*. Here it is clear that Stammler speaks with his own voice, not with the voice of the "socialist" he introduces on p. 51, *seq*.

4. On the meaning of "materialist" in the work of Marx, see Max Adler, "Kausalität und Teleologie im Streit um die Wissenschaft," *Marx Studien*, volume 1, p. 108, note 1; p. 111 (a sound criticism of Stammler); p. 116, note 1, and many other passages.

5. Unless otherwise noted, I am responsible for the interpolations between quotations from Stammler's work.

6. "Theoretical": in other words, *after* the state of affairs which *qualifies* as "a cure" and as "progress" is identified. Then the question of whether it is "possible" to produce this state of affairs and the question of whether a development approximating this state of affairs—progress—can be identified are purely factual issues. In principle, their resolution lies within the domain of empirical science.

7. Stammler offers the following example at the top of p. 71. "*In the final analysis*," economic conditions have the "decisive" influence upon the development of architecture. A parenthetical note: considered on its own merits, this illustration is hardly convincing. More important, the illustration—which represents an attempt at *empirical* confirmation—is inconsistent with the alleged "formal" character of the principle. The characteristic style of imprecision mentioned above is also apparent here. The import of expressions like "dependence" and "decisive influence" makes it possible for Stammler to retreat by employing the following evasive tactic: unlike the "strict materialist," he is making no claims about *exclusive* economic determination. But the expression "in the final analysis" has the authentic ring of historical materialism. It is too genuine, too close to the doctrine itself, to be useful for this particular maneuver.

8. I do not mean "finally" in the sense that this account even pretends to approximate an *exhaustive* enumeration of concepts of "nature." It is not a full account of logically possible concepts of "nature." Nor is it even a complete enumeration of concepts of "nature" which are in fact employed. On this point, see p. 110, *seq.*, and p. 172, *seq.*, of this essay.

9. At this point, we shall not take up the question of whether the imperative is *necessarily* "general."

10. Consider "rules" in the sense of *ethical* norms. It is obvious that they are not *logically* restricted to the domain of the "social." It is logically *possible* for "Robinson" to act "immorally" too. Compare, for example, paragraph 175 of the German Code of Criminal Law, the second case, which is concerned with a moral norm for the preservation of law.

11. Concerning the logical content of the "idealtype," see Max Weber, "Die 'Objektivität' sozialwissenschäftlicher und sozialpolitischer

Erkenntnis," *Archiv für Sozialwissenschaft und Sozialpolitik*, volume 19 (1904). See the section of the essay entitled "The Logical Structure of Idealtypical Conceptual Schemes."

12. The reader will hopefully excuse this remark. Like other remarks which follow, its triviality borders on the excessive. Remarks of this sort are necessary in order to refute certain of Stammler's arguments that have a pronounced ad hominem character.

13. At this point we are still very far from any idea of a "legal" order. Further, it is obvious that several versions—perhaps many different versions—of the *ideal* "meaning" of an act of "exchange" could eventually be constructed.

14. Consider this first analysis of the "meaning" of the act of exchange. The "meaning" of the exchange is construed as a "normative maxim" which "regulates the relationship" between the two exchange partners. Suppose that the *relationship* between the two partners is described as "governed" *by* a "norm" which they acknowledge as obligatory for their future *conduct*. Notice that the words "regulate" and "govern" do not necessarily imply subsumption under a general "rule." The only limited sense in which this is the case is the following: these words express the general "rule" that "the agreement should be kept in good faith." But this means nothing more than the following: "The rule should be treated as a rule." In order to participate in the act of exchange, the two partners require absolutely no knowledge of the general, ideal "nature" of the norm of exchange. We might even suppose that two persons could perform an act of the following description: the "meaning" that each associates with the act is absolutely idiosyncratic and not—like the "exchange"—subsumable under a general type. In other words: There is no sense in which the concept "rule-governed" *logically* presupposes the idea of *general* "rules" of a specific content. For the present, we shall only make this point. In the interests of simplicity, we shall discuss in the ensuing the sense in which a normative regulation generally implies a subsumption under "general rules."

15. In this regard, the "presuppositions" in question are *logically* analogous to the "laws" of economic theory.

16. The concept of "culture" employed here is due to Heinrich Rickert, *Die Grenzen der naturwissenschaftlichen Begriffsbildung,*

Tübingen, 1902 (chap. 4, sections 2 and 8). At this point–before criticizing Stammler's views on these issues–I shall deliberately refrain from introducing the concept of "social life." This discussion rests on ideas developed in several of my essays ("Die 'Objektivität' sozialwissenschaftlicher und sozialpolitischer Erkenntnis," *Archiv für Sozialwissenschaft und Sozialpolitik*, volume 19, 1904; "Kritische Studien auf dem Gebiet der kulturwissenschaftlichen Logik," *Archiv für Sozialwissenschaft und Sozialpolitik*, volume 22, 1906).

17. It is obvious that the norms of skat would have precisely the same status *if* some phenomenon regulated by the laws of skat became an object of investigation that interested us from the perspectives of "universal history."

18. See the penetrating remarks which Georg Jellinek has devoted to this problem (*System der subjektiven öffentlichen Rechte*, Tübingen, 1905, chap. 3, p. 12, *seq.*; *Allgemeine Staatslehre*, 2nd edition, Berlin, 1905, chap. 6). Unlike our own interest in this problem, which is grounded in "cultural theory," Jellinek's interest is grounded in law. His concern is to check naturalistic incursions into the domain of legal dogmatics or jurisprudence. Our concern is to criticize the falsification of *empirical* concepts by jurisprudence. Consider the problem of the fundamental logic of the relationship between empirical and legal thought. At this point, only one person has provided a trenchant analysis of this problem from the perspective of empirical thought: Friedrich Gottl. His book *Die Herrschaft des Wortes* (Jena, 1901) contains suggestions on this problem that are very good indeed. But they are no more than suggestions. It is well known that in his own time Böhm-Bawerk offered a consistently clear discussion of legally protected interests ("subjective rights"), especially from the standpoint of economic thought. See his treatise *Rechte und Verhältnisse vom Standpunkt der volkswirtschaftlichen Güterlehre*, 1881.

19. This is an extravagant oversimplification.

20. See also Gottl, *Die Herrschaft des Wortes* (Jena, 1901), p. 192, note 1, and the pages which follow.

21. This is based on the following purely factual consideration: the significance of the "rules of skat" for cultural life is very limited.

22. I shall not undertake here an analysis of the *empirical* content of the facts that correspond to these concepts.

23. From a logical standpoint, the conceptual apparatus employed in the "history of law" is certainly not as easy to classify as it might at first appear. We shall only note this point in passing. Let us examine the following question. *Empirically*, what does it mean to claim that a certain body of law was "valid" during a certain period? Consider the fact that a legal principle expressed in certain symbols and imprinted in printer's ink is found in a certain volume that is handed down to us as a "code of law." This source of knowledge, which is sometimes completely inaccessible, is an extremely important piece of evidence germane to the answer to this question. But it is not necessarily the only decisive piece of evidence. Moreover this fact *invariably* requires "interpretation" and "application" to the concrete case at issue. And the status of this concrete case may be problematical. From the standpoint of the history of law, perhaps the logical "import" of the "validity" of this body of law could be expressed in the following hypothetical proposition. *Suppose* that a "jurist" of that time *had* undertaken to decide a conflict of interest according to certain rules of law. And suppose we knew—from whatever sources—that certain principles of legal reasoning had a predominant influence during this period. And *suppose*, finally, that this decision was made in accordance with these principles of legal reasoning. Then a decision with a certain import *would have been expected* with a very high degree of *probability*.

Consider the following two questions. How "would" the judge in fact have decided the case? And how *should* the judge have decided the case? We are all too easily inclined to pose the latter question instead of the former. In that case, we impose a dogmatic construction upon an empirical inquiry. In view of the following considerations, it is very difficult to resist this inclination. (a) In fact, such a construction is *essential* as an "heuristic device." We regularly proceed, quite unintentionally, in the following way. First we interpret the historical "sources of law" of our own time dogmatically. And then, to the extent that this is possible or necessary, we "test" the historical-empirical validity of our interpretation against the "facts" (precedents handed down to us, etc.).

(b) Further, we are often obliged—indeed, we are *usually* obliged—to employ *our own* interpretation for descriptive purposes in order to reach any conclusions at all concerning the "validity" of an earlier law. Otherwise an intelligible and coherent account of the earlier law would simply be impossible. The reasons for this are as follows. Either an unequivocal and internally consistent legal concept was not in fact developed at the time. Or such a concept was not generally accepted at the time (consider the concept of *"Gewere"*—"secure possession" or "protection"—in certain medieval sources). In this last case, it is obvious that we must make a very careful attempt to determine the extent to which the possible "theory" or "theories" which *we* develop correspond to the empirical "legal consciousness" of the historical period in question. Our own "theories" are useful only as a provisional, classificatory scheme. But consider the "legal consciousness" of this particular historical period. There is no reason at all to believe that it was necessarily unambiguous. And it is even less likely that it was internally consistent. In every case, we employ our dogmatic constructions as "idealtypes," in the sense of this expression that I have explained elsewhere. A conceptual construct of this sort is never the *conclusion* or the *product* of an empirical investigation. On the contrary, it is invariably either an heuristic *technique* or a *means* of description (or both).

Consider, in view of the foregoing and from the standpoint of the history of law, a "rule of law" the *empirical* "validity" of which had been established—in other words, a law that is *empirically* "valid" within a certain spatio-temporally defined period of history. Such a "rule of law" also functions as an "idealtype" of the *actual* behavior of the persons who potentially fall under its jurisdiction. We begin with the probability that the *actual* behavior of the contemporaries of this period conformed to this "legal rule" at least to a certain degree. Wherever possible and necessary, we "empirically verify" the hypothesis that a corresponding "maxim of legality" can be attributed to the contemporaries of this period. Both the frequent substitution of "rules of law" for empirical "regularities" and the use of legal terms to describe economic facts are based on these considerations.

24. And he does this in spite of that fact that in *Kant Studien*, volume 1, Vorländer pointed out that Stammler "misunderstood" these

illustrations. However what Vorländer interprets as "misunderstanding" is actually the scrupulous avoidance of clarity on the part of Stammler.

25. As stated, this point is radically mistaken. It creates the impression that the authentic function of causal inquiry is not the production of generalizations and that value judgments could not be oriented to concrete, individual entities.

26. Of course it remains unclear whether Stammler conceives this "idea" as *our* idea or as an empirical *object*. We are all too familiar with the obscurity that surrounds Stammler's discussion of this point. Consider, moreover, the following problem. If an "idea" is not included in the "domain" of "nature," then how can an "instinct" be included within this "domain"? An "instinct" is no more "observable" than an "idea." Further, it is obviously not only the "instincts" of others that we can "empathize with" (see Stammler, p. 340). On the contrary, in the strict sense, this is possible only in the case of another person's "ideas." Finally, these claims concerning *empathy* with the "instinctual life" of another person do not prevent Stammler from making a reference—at the bottom of the same page, 340—to the exclusively causal determination of "observable" phenomena.

27. See the section of this essay entitled "Analysis of the Concept of a Rule: The Concept of a Rule of a Game."

28. Stammler, note 51 to p. 88. On the same point, see also Stammler, p. 641.

29. See Stammler, p. 91.

30. Notice that on p. 92, paragraphs 3 and 4, Stammler introduces "consensus"—in contrast to the "life of purely instinctual drives"—as the definitive feature of social life. This distinction is, of course, completely mistaken. On p. 94, he refers to human *precepts*. Following p. 94, he says that it would be possible to acknowledge a "social existence" among *animals* only if it could be proven that in animal communities (beehives, for example) "external, observable rules of this sort were instituted *by the animals*." They are rules to which the animals themselves are alleged to conform.

31. Stammler's distinction between "morality," on the one hand, and "law" and "convention," on the other, corresponds to the usual

distinction. Consider the following question. On what grounds does a given kind of behavior fail to correspond to a legal norm? In particular, consider the interests of other persons that are protected by law. What "convictions" (deceit, blameworthy motives, good faith, error, etc.) are responsible for the violation of such a law? These questions are certainly not legally irrelevant. This point should always be kept in mind so that the logical rigor of this distinction between "morality" and "law" is not exaggerated.

32. Stammler carefully avoids the use of this expression.

33. At this point I refer to my earlier remarks and repeat: Obviously at *no* point in this critique do I impute any "crafty" or "deceitful" intentions to Stammler. However consider a second edition (!) of a work which not only permits sophisms of this sort, but is *exhaustively* and *exclusively* based upon them. Language provides no other means of describing such a *"culpa lata"*: it is a totally irresponsible lapse. When I use these expressions and others of similar severity, I only mean the following. *If* the fulfillment of scientific obligations were subject to "external, observable rules," then of course Stammler's conduct would in fact qualify as "illegal."

34. A word at this point on how Stammler uses the case of Robinson Crusoe for his own purposes (see Stammler, p. 105, *seq.*). The "first stage"—as Stammler calls it—is only constituted by the "technique or technology of Robinson's isolated economy" (note!). "Collective life governed by rules" begins at the point when Robinson "acquired Friday as a companion: when (note!) the young Indian placed the foot of the white man on his neck and, in effect, said 'you shall be my master.'" Why is this the case? *Because* at this point, in addition to questions of "technique," a second "consideration" (note!) acquires relevance "for both parties" (note!): "the social question." In other words, without that symbolic act (or some other act with the same empirically intended meaning), the (empirically intended) "import" of which was "meant" to express subjugation, "social life" would not exist. For example, this would not be the case if Robinson treated Friday like the master treats his dog: in other words, if Robinson had confined, fed, and trained ("taught") him for his own (Robinson's) purposes. Suppose that, in order to make him as useful as possible, the master, by the use of certain signs, "made the dog understand." In that case, the

master would have come to an "understanding" with his dog. Then the relationship between master and dog would be the same as the relationship between Robinson and Friday. Further, the fact that these signs would have the import of a "rule-governed order" (on this point see Stammler's remarks at the top of p. 86) holds in exactly the same sense for the "orders" the master gives to his dog. Robinson would probably also consider it in his interest to teach Friday to speak his language. In the case of the dog, of course, this is not possible. But suppose that it were. Now consider Stammler's remarks on pp. 96–97. Stammler says that language is a "primitive convention." But "convention" qualifies as "rule-governed collective life." It follows that "social life" would begin when man and dog could speak with one another. It would cease when this were no longer possible. In other words, the relationship between Robinson and Friday is no different from the relationship between the master and his dog. There are also "orders," "symbolic means of coming to an understanding," etc. between man and dog. Consider Bräsig's claim that a whipping is the best way of maintaining good relations between dog and man. It is well known that the slave holders extended this principle to the blacks. Perhaps the reader will pardon this ridiculous piece of casuistry when he reads Stammler's triumphant proclamation (p. 106). "There is no possible intermediate state between the isolated circumstances of Robinson and his regulated (note!) communal life with Friday. An intermediary stage is *inconceivable*." As a matter of fact, abstract economic theory—ridiculed by Stammler because of its predilection for Robinson Crusoe—always employed Defoe's immortal character more judiciously than our scholastic himself.

35. "It makes no sense." Of course this really only means: It "is not consistent with my (Stammler's) conceptual scheme."

36. I think there is hardly any doubt that the closely related claims that Friedrich Gottl makes about "historical" life (*Die Grenzen der Geschichte*, Leipzig, 1904) are in some respects influenced by Stammler's views. Stammler himself does not use this expression.

37. See above, p. 96, *seq.*, and p. 110, *seq.*

Index

183

137-41, 178-79n. 23
rule of, 124-42
Stammler's concept of, 37
Legal concepts and conceptual schemes
in the sociocultural sciences,
124-26, 130-31, 134-37, 179n. 23
Legal order:
Axiological or dogmatic conception
of, 129-30, 133, 139-41
concept of, 22-23, 176n. 13
empirical significance of, 129-30,
132-35, 137-41

Marx, Karl, 69, 174
Materialism, 145-46
Meaning:
and nature, 24, 110-11, 115,
172-73
and rules, 107, 176n. 14
and social life, 109-111
cultural, 40, 48n. 12
dogmatic or hypothetical constructs of, 35-36, 107, 111-15,
141
explanation of Weber's theory of,
22-38, 49n. 14
of action, 111-15

Natural science:
and social science, 2-3, 95-97, 100,
102, 104-105, 172-73
and teleological science, 150
Stammler's concept of, 145, 150,
152, 172-73
Nature, 95-97, 141, 153, 172-73,
175n. 8

Problematics and conceptual schemes:
causal or empirical, 73-74, 82-86,
141-43, 171
dogmatic, 35-36, 107, 111-15, 141,
143, 145-55, 158, 161, 171,
178-79n. 23
teleological, 121-22, 142, 145-55

Rickert, Heinrich, vii-ix, 6-7, 29,
41-43, 44-45, 54, 176n. 16
Robinson Crusoe:
and economic rules, 99-100, 102,
104-107, 110-11
and Stammler's concept of social
life, 162-63, 175n. 10, 181-82n.
34

Rules:
analysis of, 50n. 16, 99-103
and causes, 119
and laws of nature, 98
as empirical maxims, 98-99,
104-107, 112-18, 122-23
as norms, 34, 98-99, 105-108,
112-23, 175n. 10, 176n. 14
as presuppositions, 119-24
as the subject matter of social science, 3, 98-99
critique of Stammler's view of,
99-100, 102, 141-42
of a game, 22-23, 34, 115-24
validity of, 99, 160-61, 174

Social life:
and language, 164-65
and nature, 38n. 1, 95-98, 172
and precepts, 158-59, 161-69, 173
and rules, 3, 98-99, 108-109, 131,
136-37, 155-74
Stammler's concept of, 2-3, 38n. 1,
92, 94-98, 155-74

Teleology:
and nature, 38n. 1
as a kind of science, 150
as a problematic, 82-86, 145-55
critique of Stammler's view of, 37
Theory of knowledge:
critique of Stammler's view of,
71-78
Stammler's view of, 68-71

Validity:
and causation, 148-49
axiological, 75, 84-85, 128-29, 131,
161, 171
dogmatic, 160
empirical, 73, 75, 127-30, 137,
140, 178-79n. 23
ideal, 108, 114-15, 118, 125, 128,
130, 160, 174
logical, 75
universal and unconditional, 70, 73,
77
Values:
and relevance, 121-22
and value judgments, 84-86, 98
as the domain of axiology, 74-75,
85-86, 97